PRESENTED TO:

CONTENTS

From Point Guard to Prophet

BY

Sophia Ruffin

LIFE TO LEGACY

From Point Guard to Prophet
Sophia Ruffin
Copyright ©2016

ISBN-13: 978-1-939654-76-2
ISBN-10: 1-939654-76-9

Scripture quotations are taken from the Authorized King James Version.

Printed in the United States
10 9 8 7 6 5 4 3 2 1

Cover concept by: DeAnna Crudup

Cover design by: Traneisha Y. Jones

Published by
Life To Legacy, LLC
P.O. Box 57
Blue Island, IL 60406
877-267-7477
www.Life2Legacy.com
Life2legacybooks@att.net

DEDICATION

$\mathcal{I}$ would like to dedicate this book to the Holy Spirit, who inspired me to write this book in ten days. It is my desire that Jesus be exalted and lifted up throughout these pages. May the Holy Spirit break out in a tangible way, allowing you, the reader, to enter into a real, intimate relationship with my deliverer, who is open and ready to deliver you. I would also like to dedicate this book to my loving parents, Lindsey Ruffin and Doris Hodo, who brought me forth in the earth.

To my mother who labored with me, walked me through deliverance, believed in me, and loved me through my sin. You played a key role in my deliverance and your love covered a multitude of my sin. Thank you for being an example of a woman of God who overcame adversity, put pride to the side, and loved me unconditionally through the good, bad and ugly. You are my best friend, you are my joy, and you are a blessing. Thank you mom for trusting the mandate on my life and for never giving up on me. Dad, I love you and appreciate you. Thank you for being my friend and always knowing what to say to put a smile on my face. I have witnessed you grow, overcome your personal adversities, and rise into an awesome man. You've always accepted me for who I am, and your love towards me is unquestionable.

To my grandmother, thank you for being such a woman of grace, love and beauty. You have paved the foundation of the prophetic in the bloodline, and I'm so blessed to have received the mantle. Thank you to my host of aunts, uncles, and cousins.

To my siblings, I love y'all beyond words. I am so thankful for my sister who loves me with a love that never fails. You helped me during my most vulnerable years. Thank you for never giving up on me. To my brother, I love you and thank you for always having my back, and being the best brother in the world. I'm blessed to have grown up with both of you. I also send my thanks to my brother-in-law, and my nieces and nephews. Thank you, Marquese Hodo, for believing in auntie and pushing me to strive for success.

To my god-momma LaKenia Robinson, who has been a second mother during my most vulnerable years when I needed you most. You been rocking with me since day one, I love you.

To my best friend Devon Mays, thank you for walking me through the fire and sticking by my side through the midst of adversity, obstacles, and persecution. Thank you for the endless nights of praying, fasting, covering, protecting, supporting, and believing in me. Thank you for the strength after the altar as you pushed and walked me through my deliverance, and helped me launch into womanhood. To the girls, I love you both.

I also send a word of thank you to Apostle Tim and Kelley Brinson for walking me through deliverance and discipleship. Special shout out to Momma Lil, for teaching me how to war.

To the host of leaders God has brought in my life to play a key role in my destiny, I appreciate you all. Pastor Lydia Clark for believing in me, and ordaining me. Apostle Lance and Traci Delashment for covering me, Bernice Holiday for fighting for me, Veronica Crim for mentoring me, and Mother Shummate for being a midwife. I love you all dearly.

I want to thank my favorite teacher in the entire world, Annie Flowers, the woman who spoke life, purpose, and destiny into my life. May your legacy remain, I am so grateful for you.

Lastly, I would like to thank each of you for being a blessing. Crystal Banks, Tameeka Williams, Beverly Wade, Kischa Jackson, Sabena Greer, Kelley Taylor, Erica Williams, Taylor Holland, Chaundria Zeigler, Tiffiny Payton, Chowee & Tara Thomas, Crystal Wiggins, Sister Verona Fran Monroe, and Janice Henderson. Thank you, Michelle Wilson, for being a divine, kingdom connection.

PRAYER

I pray that as you open this book, you will be met by the presence of the Most High God. I prophesy that the words of my story will be a highlight and compliment of the power of God. May this book demonstrate the pen of a ready writer inspired by the unction of the Holy Ghost. I declare that emphasis of the power of God will be articulated in a way that will shake the powers of darkness and unleash the presence of the kingdom. May your heart be open, sober, willing, and ready to receive the tangible presence of the Lord. Even as I commend these words to the Holy Spirit, I declare that the spirit will break out upon you throughout the course of your reading. I prophesy that you will be hit with power from page one, and will pause to give God a shout of praise, that will overthrow your enemies. I declare that your spirit will be awakened, and you will see the blueprint of heaven's agenda concerning your destiny. May you be restored, renewed, delivered and set free from the pain and residue of your past. I declare that childhood rejection, abandonment, and trauma be uprooted, and the power of God be applied. I declare that your feebleness would be strengthened and that your heart would be awakened with a passion, zeal, thrust and yearning to go after God like never before. I declare that the winds of heaven would blow upon the pages, and the presence of God and all His power would sit upon you during your time of reading. I declare that this book will restore families, heal the broken child, give hope to the grieving parent, and bring knowledge to those who have been affected by the deceptions of the enemy regarding the spirit of homosexuality. I prophesy that by the end of this book, the enemy will have no grip on you regarding whatever spirit with which you are wrestling. In Jesus Name. Amen.

FOREWORD

$\mathcal{W}$alking into a gymnasium and walking into a church were two totally different extremes for me. Noise, screaming, cheering, shouting, rooting one on, sweating, hustling, diving, high-fiving, fist bumping, offense, and defense. Yes, my type of atmosphere! When you walk into a gym, you can literally smell the aroma of strawberry perfume and sweat dripping, and you are instantly charged by the atmosphere. The gym was the place to be. I loved and lived for this scene. Basketball was my life and my identity. It was in my DNA and the essence of my being. I was convinced that I was put on this earth to play ball, and to be a part of the sports and entertainment arena. Running the point, setting the tempo, and leading my team to victory was my motivation. Uplifting the team when defeated, being the floor general, visionary, and playmaker ran deep in my blood. I was built for this, and my heart burned for the game. My tongue thirsted for more, so I chased my dream of playing professional basketball and like a deer that pants after water, my soul longed for the game. The only arena and platform

I ever yearned for was a shiny wooden floor, with WNBA painted across the hardwood, two 10 foot high, 18 inch rims at opposite ends of the court, with crispy nets that snap like a whip when my three pointers hit the bottom of the net.

Oh, how I burned to crossover opponents, oppositions, and any enemy that stood in my way. I worshipped the game; it came before anything and anyone. Basketball was my beginning and my end. I bowed down and worshipped the game, tattooed the word sacrifice across my leg with prayer hands, and declared in my heart that no matter what it took I would risk it all for the game. I studied my opponents, and I modeled myself after greats like Cynthia Cooper, Lisa Leslie, and Sheryl Swoopes. My hands sweated and yearned to grip a Wilson leather ball, so I ran after my vision with my eyes fixed on making it to the big league. I prepared for the big moment of one day being introduced as the face of the WNBA, and I couldn't wait to sit at the table and sign my national letter of intent to a major university. I could hear Dick Vitale commentating and saying my name all over ESPN. My dream was so tangible, and the enemy allowed me to physically touch the very desires of my heart. I could feel it, so I sprinted after the tangible presence of making my dream a reality. Although I wasn't the greatest player; I knew the day would come when I would rise up and be the face of the game I loved.

THEN THIS HAPPENED...

Church? What! God! Who...Wait, hold up! Plans for my life? A prophet to the nations? What nations? Prophet what? How could this be? You mean to tell me basketball wasn't my future. Hold up God, you're making a huge mistake. What do you mean you have plans for my life? I can't live any other way. I'm unlearned, unskilled, and untrained, how can you use me for your kingdom? What kingdom? Basketball is the kingdom I want to function in. I spent years investing all I had in this game. I trained for this plan. I spent countless hours working out, training, 3 a.m. workouts, conditioning, and training my mind and emotions for the game, and you mean to tell me just like that, you have a different plan? This has to be a practical joke, right? Wake up Sophia; this is only a nightmare. God calling you is not a dream; this is some type of sick, twisted nightmare.

There is no way I can be a prophet to anyone's nation when I'm not even fit to be a prophet to the person next to me. I spent endless hours, all my life, devising my own plan and you mean to tell me you're going to walk right into my life and change the game. You are going to change the course of my life and my destiny just like that? God hold up, I thought you said; "you would give me the desires of my heart." Basketball is my desire, this is what I long to do, I prepared for this. I'm not a prophet. I don't know what to say or what to do. How can you use me after I've spent years betraying you, turning my back on you, and rebelling against you? I don't even really know you. How can you use me, I'm only a child?

What about my lifestyle, how can you use me—I'm gay? I like girls, therefore, I'm unclean, right? This has got to be a nightmare. I'm so unworthy of you even speaking to me, and you're talking about using me.

"Confusion gripped my heart until God responded."

"The game has suddenly changed for you, daughter. I had a plan for you before the foundations of the world, and it can't be altered or reversed. Before I formed you in your mother's womb, I separated you and set you apart, consecrating you, and ordaining you to be a prophet to the nations. I called you unto myself. You are mine, and I am yours. I am a jealous lover over your soul, and the time has come for me to bring you closer to me. You had a plan, but my plan prevails. I called you my child, and you are my beloved in whom I'm well pleased. I'm going to use your story. Fear not, for you are not only a child, you are a prophet to the nations. You are the comeback kid, and I will use you to snatch others out of the fire. You are a game changer, and I allowed you to rise in the arena of sports, and to comprehend naturally the role of a point guard, so that you would understand the function of a prophet. You learned submission early, you learned leadership, and you grasped the concept of a coach-player relationship. You learned to drown out the noises and distractions, and you have a heart of love.

Now is the time I will change the game, and I will now give you the desires of My heart. Will you burn for me daughter? Will you go for me daughter? Will you rise and be My ambassador in the Earth? I am your coach, and I shall personally orchestrate My plans through you. I will give you access to the kingdom, and will release My words to you. You shall go out before all the nations and announce My words over the Earth. You shall speak from the embassy of heaven, and I will reveal My heart to you. I will take you places that basketball could never have taken you. I will cause you to pioneer a brand new move. Rise up Sophia, it's now your time. And I shall give you strength to not only slay the Goliath of homosexuality, but you shall also cut off the head and take the sword. Come back, go forth throughout the earth, and share the goodness of Jesus. I am with you every step of the way. Vengeance is mine says the Lord, and hell will pay the price for touching my very elect. Fear not for I am with you.

CHAPTER 1
CHILDHOOD DREAM

Before I formed thee in the belly I knew thee, and before thou
camest forth out of the womb I sanctified thee, and I ordained
thee a prophet unto the nations.
Jeremiah 1:5

*G*rowing up, I was always told that the American
dream of attending college, getting married, having two
kids- a boy and a girl, a house with a white picket fence and
a dog, equaled success. For some reason, I always bucked the
American dream. It never really settled in my spirit and as a
child, I was determined to create my own measure of success.
I hated rules and formulas, and I was always seeking ways
to invent, create, and implement my own thing. Of course, I
valued education and family, but I didn't agree with the system America used to define success.

Thinking back to when I was a little girl, I can recall
family members and teachers asking, "Sophia, what do you

want to be when you grow up?"Without hesitation, and with three ponytails, bangs, a gap in my teeth, and a huge smile, I would clench my fist, and scream as I looked them straight in the eyes and said, " I'm going to be the first female to make it to the NBA." Back in the day, the WNBA was not in existence, so I had decided to pursue my dream of being an NBA star until a women's league came into existence. Confusion and total disbelief would fall on the faces of many of my family members and teachers. They would respond by saying, "You need to pick another dream," shake their heads, and proceed to say, " that don't make any sense, that girl is just bad." Teachers would say Sophia write something else down, but I refused, so for years they called me hard-headed and rebellious. Deep in my heart there was nothing else I could envision myself doing. At an early age, my mind was set on exactly what I wanted to be and how I was going to achieve it. Many made fun of my idea of success.

The American dream wasn't my blueprint. I desired to be the architect of my own destiny; and it was my passion to design, create, build and implement my own path of success. I learned how to dream big, shoot for the stars and go after exactly what I wanted. Growing up, I heard about the American dream, but to be honest, not many people in my family lived the dream they were trying to tell me to live. It's funny because the only impression of the American dream that I saw was on television. *The Cosby Show* was the only representation of an African-American family living the American dream, and that wasn't realistic for my life. Although

The Cosby Show was an amazing show, it wasn't achievable in my environment, so I decided to create Sophia's dream and become the first one in my family to be successful by taking my own path of success. Basketball was my way out, and it was my blueprint to reach the level of success I that yearned.

Growing up, I always felt there was something different about me. I was considered the wild child, the bad seed. I always found myself doing the opposite of what I was told. Many would call my behavior rebellious. I was often misunderstood, mishandled, and rejected. I hated being inside a box so anytime a system or structure tried to box me in, I always broke out. Because I refused to follow the traditional American idea of a dream, I was forced to create my own. I was a young innovator, and I learned to introduce new methods and ideas. I always wanted to introduce something new, and make changes in anything that appeared to be established. That was my personality. Whatever I wanted, I created it to be.

THE STIGMA

I am the youngest of three siblings, and we are all different in so many ways. While we each have our own personalities, the one thing we do share is a love for one another that's beyond words. Although I had two older siblings, I never wanted to follow their plan or footsteps, so I created my own. My sister Alison was a cheerleader and pom-pom player. She also ran track, and OMG she was and still is the prettiest woman to walk the earth. She carried herself as a lady, was a girly girl, and every boy on the block wanted to date her. My brother Lindsey was a football star. He was very popular, and for years, I walked in his shadow as Lindsey's little sister. He was well known everywhere we went, and to be honest, we fought on a daily basis, but he didn't allow anyone else to mess with me. He was my protector, my brother.

One evening around 9 p.m. we were walking home from New Fellowship Church in Chicago Heights. The previous pastor was Pastor Jones, and he was a strong believer in outreach ministry and creating an atmosphere to bring in people off the streets. Because of this, he opened the church during the week for the young people to come in and play basketball in the gym. The catch was that in order to play, you first had to attend Bible Study. We were faithful in attending because we wanted to play basketball. I was always one of the only girls to play with grown men, and I would get picked to play before most of the boys my age. My brother would be so hard on me, yelling and telling me to go hard. I think the men were afraid to foul me because they knew my brother would beat them up if they attacked me too hard, so I had an advantage.

Okay, let me move forward into my thoughts, see even in writing a book, I tend to get distracted. Oh, so yall know, my sister would just sit pretty, and watch us play. This particular night we were walking home, which was like eight blocks away. While we were walking, it was raining, pitch black, and darkness permeated the atmosphere. The three of us were walking and talking loud. We were joking and making fun of people, and just having a good time. All of a sudden, I looked down on the ground, and it was full of night crawlers. These worms were everywhere. I screamed, jumped, and tried to dodge stepping on one. However, it was impossible due to so many being on the ground. I stopped right in front of a nursing home. Cars zoomed past us, and for a second it felt like my life just paused. I cried, jumped up and down, and said I'm not walking anymore. I refused to take another step. My brother screamed, "Moochie you better come on." He knew that he couldn't leave me, and couldn't go home without me, so he yelled at me repeatedly. He was so mad and kept saying "bring your scary butt on." I refused to move. My sister laughed her pretty little heart out. Finally, my brother walked toward me and said, "Come on." He bent down and carried me all the way home on his back. He was so mad. He talked about me, and cursed me out the entire walk, but underneath his frustration, he showed so much love because he carried me all the way home. My brother was my backbone. I can tell so many stories of my siblings, but this one stands out the most.

Even though athletics ran in our family, I didn't want to cheer, run track, or play football, so I picked up basketball. I began playing with my brother as a child. He was very competitive, and we would go into the basement, take a sock and a laundry basket, and literally play one-on-one for hours. We would go hard in the basement, using whatever we had tangibly to create the atmosphere we needed to play the game we both loved. After playing with socks, we would take the laundry and shoot hoops by throwing the white load into the washer machine.

When we got tired of shooting hoops with dirty clothes, we would take a crate, hang it on the wall outside and play ball. We did that for years until my parents were able to afford to get us a basketball rim. When we finally got the basketball rim, we would play in the driveway for hours. We would even pull the rim into the middle of the street, and one of the neighbors would bring his rim, and we would play full court right in the middle of the street.

Hilltop Avenue was the place to be, until our neighbor Ms. Daisy came home. When this woman came home, and the rims were blocking a smooth transition for her to pull up in the driveway, all the kids knew it was about to go down. This woman was so respected, and she was the general of the block. She didn't have to utter a word. We just knew to pave the way because Ms. Daisy is coming home. When her car turned the corner, we would hustle to move the courts out of the street so that she could pull into the yard without hesitation. The more we showed her respect, the easier she was on us kids by allowing us to continue the game without running us off. Ms. Daisy was a huge basketball fan, and whenever you saw her, she would be rocking a Bulls jacket, Bulls shirt, Bulls hat, and if they had Bulls sneakers, she would have those on too. She was the realest old woman on the block. Ms. Daisy was a "G".

Back then, basketball was only played for fun, but suddenly the game that was fun began turning into something else. When you saw Sophia, you saw a ball in my hand! I ate with that ball, slept with my ball & everywhere I went I was sure to represent basketball. My identity was being marked, and the enemy was taking my pure joy and innocence away by launching the missile of homosexuality. My gender identity was coming under attack. I didn't know anything about lesbianism. I was just hooping. Suddenly, the loud noise of adults sitting on their porches, driving by in their cars, and whispering to their daughters to stay away from me because I was gay began to permeate the atmosphere. I would go home, wash my face, look in the mirror, and say to myself, " Gay, am I gay?" The seed of lesbianism was suddenly planted when so many adults began attaching my athletic ability to my sexuality and proclaiming that I was a lesbian. The stigma of me playing basketball began with a foreign seed of their words calling me gay. Like cancer, what began in my mind, began spreading all over my body at a fast pace with the intent to kill me. Homosexuality was like cancer in my life. I didn't know I had it until it was diagnosed. However, it laid dormant inside me until the opportune time of manifestation.

My mother couldn't stand the fact that I played basketball, especially after she got wind of others linking my athletic ability to being gay. Now she was suspicious and would look me upside my head, trying to figure out what was going on. She was caught between the opinion of others making comments and putting pressure on her by making little comments about her baby. It wasn't the game that my mother hated, it was the stigma associated with it that she couldn't handle.

She was trying to protect my reputation that was being gunned down like an innocent victim caught in a drive-by shooting. She tried to cover me, and didn't know what to do, so trying to stop me from playing basketball was her method to stop the bullets from shooting at my reputation. I was beginning to panic because all I wanted to do was play ball, now I was worried about what people thought about me, and how I was being perceived. Now playing basketball was taking on a whole new meaning, and because the enemy doesn't play fair, he was in full motion towards slowly pushing me into his agenda of using me as a principality for the power of darkness.

I became aware of the fact that I was different. When I began playing basketball, I didn't see myself as a lesbian; I only saw myself as a tomboy. Being a tomboy was acceptable and appropriate, because many girls began as tomboys, and become the cutest girly girls ever. The enemy wasn't satisfied with me thinking I was a tomboy; he wanted me to swallow the words that I was gay. I began focusing on me being different and went on this quest of trying to find my identity. Every time I looked in the mirror, I would say I am ugly, I am a boy, I'm gay, I like girls, and the words of others would replay loudly in my ears until they became a melody that I sang over myself. I wasn't like every other girl; there was something different about me. While all of the girls on my block were jumping rope, playing with dolls and wearing skirts, I would be in the middle of the street with a ball in my hand, practicing how to dribble between my legs. I was working on my handles, and perfecting my ball handling ability. The girls would even cheer me on, and watch me dribble, sweat, and perform my rendition of a ball player smack dead in the street. One day my mother pulled up in the car, she rolled down the window, and the look on her face was one of fury. I immediately thought to myself, what's wrong, so I decided to make her day by smiling excitedly, and saying, " Look, mom, I learned how to dribble the ball between my legs." My mother got very upset; I had struck a nerve that sent her to the red zone of anger. She looked at me, and said in a fierce tone, " You better go put that ball up right now and pick up a rope. Why can't you go over there with the girls and do what they are doing?" My mother was beginning to hate the fact that her little girl was turning out to be like one of the boys, and she felt that if she could get the ball out of my hand, I would be more lady like, but it was too late. I had already fallen in love with the game and had already digested the words of the enemy that declared I wasn't like other girls, I was different, and I was gay. The foreign object of demonic words was planted deep in my mind and heart. I was now on a quest to discover the voice I heard the loudest, and that was the voice of the enemy speaking to me in great detail.

The moment I realized my mother disapproved of me playing basketball, something on the inside pushed me to pursue the game even more. I was 11 years old when it all began. In grade school, I wasn't able to play organized basketball because they didn't offer sports until junior high. Although my mother disapproved of me playing, I tried out for the girls' basketball team anyway. Sixth grade, Calumet Junior High School, I can remember it like it was yesterday. I was walking through the halls and going through the tunnels from class to class, as I saw signs hung on the wall stating Girls' Basketball Tryouts today after school. Excitement, joy, and great anticipation filled my heart. All I kept saying throughout the day was, " I'm trying out for the team, you trying out." I ran around asking peer after peer, " Are you trying out? I can't wait because I know I'm going to make it." I had confidence out of this world. I wasn't intimidated or afraid; I just knew I was already on the team.

On the day of tryouts, I walked into the gym with my long tube socks, low top sneakers, baggy shorts, T-shirt, and a headband. All the other girls were stretching and appeared to be nervous. They were dressed neatly in their attire, some had long hair and were girly girls, so I automatically assumed and said to myself, I can beat her. I connected being good in basketball with being a tomboy. Most of the girls who were more feminine weren't taken seriously when it came to the game. Although they were good, they just weren't respected on the level of the more masculine girls. I didn't hesitate, and definitely didn't think about stretching. I grabbed a ball off the rack and started shooting threes. Airball after airball, but I didn't care I was shooting and talking junk. I was dribbling the ball between my legs, and losing the ball. I was completely out-of-control, but in my mind, I felt unstoppable.

The coach smiled and just shook her head at me. She was impressed with my tenacity, zeal, passion, and of course my cockiness. She shook her head, and grabbed the ball saying, "You a little cocky little thing." I laughed, and said, "Yeah." When the tryout began, I was the loudest, trash talking young person in the gym. Missed layup after missed layup, however, my passion confidence and attitude caused me to have favor with the coach. I made the team, and immediately I noticed something different about me. I had a funny feeling in my stomach. I couldn't put my finger on it, but I knew it was something different. The coach was a tall lady, very masculine, short hair, light brown complexion, and many of the girls and boys would make comments that the coach was gay. Then I noticed, uh oh there was that word again, gay.

We didn't really know what it meant, but we knew she was gay based on her appearance, masculinity, and the way she carried herself. She was different from the other female teachers. As a matter of fact, every female gym teacher I had, looked different from the other women. They all had a form of masculinity about themselves, and the kids would call them gay. I even overheard other teachers calling my coach a lesbian. I was now connecting the dots that maybe all women who are masculine, and have a connection with sports is gay, especially basketball. So I immediately connected because I was called gay, lesbian, and told I would be gay, so I wanted to know more about this gay stuff.

All the girls on the team would say yuck that's nasty, she likes girls. They would whisper and say that their mother's told them not to be around Coach D because she was a dike. I was learning new vocabulary, and for some reason, I hated to hear people use the words dike and butch. As I sat there listening to the girls, I was confused because I couldn't understand why I wasn't disgusted. I was actually drawn to Coach D and would defend her whenever other teachers talked about her. Whatever it was about her, I wanted to learn more. Many of the boys would call me tomboy or would say I was gay, and one girl said I was a butch like her mother had said. I would even get into fights with my peers because they would call me names. My only weapon of defense was to fight. I got into multiple fights, with boys and girls, whoever came after me with an attack concerning my sexuality. I fought vehemently, with everything in me. After whooping on so many people, I was no longer confronted with bullying out loud, so clicks formed and they would whisper.

I became one of Coach D's favorite players. She would make comments like, "that's my girl," would sing my praises and would always pat me on the butt. One of the girls would say we shouldn't pat each other on the butt, but the coach would say, it's basketball, it's ok. Things started to get weird really quick. One day we had to try on uniforms, and the coach wanted us to come inside her office to try them on individually. The girls were looking at one another, some were afraid and confused, so they would whisper asking why she was making them go into her office one at a time to undress. I sat there like a little champ. When it was my turn, I smiled, laughed, and boldly walked into the office undressed, and tried on my uniform. The coach would say, "That's my girl." It was something about her affirmation and approval that captured my mind, my heart, and my imagination. Although my coach never touched me or said anything directly towards me, it was the affirmation that kept me drawn to her. I sought after her words of approval, and my young soul longed for more of her words. My feelings for Coach D turned into a crush, and in an instant, I had my gaze fixated on a woman. I didn't know what to do with these feelings and desires. So I bottled them up and attempted to suppress these strange affections that were screaming within for this curious new passion.

I began to find an excuse to get in my coach's presence; I did anything possible to seek her attention because I thirsted for her words of approval and affirmation. The more she praised me, the harder I went in practice and on the court because her praises were the song and tune of my heart. Sixth grade is when I began to discover same-sex attraction. My attraction was towards someone older, and not towards any of my peers. The stigma of homosexuality and basketball became my new truth. The enemy crept in early, and began to set the stage, and open the door to the spirit of homosexuality. Basketball was his agenda to launch his demonic grenade towards my destiny. When the door was opened in sixth grade, it began to burst open even wider. In the midst of me pursuing my dream, the enemy had already unleashed his attack.

So the journey begins... 11 years old, confused, scared,

uncertain, and desperate to play basketball, all while trying to discover my identity. At 11 years old I was so fragile and lost, afraid of all the mixed feelings I had about myself as well as others. I was vulnerable, and screaming for help. Although I was rebellious and my behavior demonstrated leave me alone, it was my inner cry for help. Yet, instead of receiving help, I was driven further and further into a state of confusion.

On a weekly basis, someone would release these words in my ear by calling me a dike, butch, man or lesbian. I had a male cousin who would faithfully take the time to get in front of a crowd and openly comment, "You a little man. Hey everybody, look at this little man." "Moochie you a little man," over and over. I swallowed, and I digested his comments like food to the soul. Those words tormented me. I was ashamed, embarrassed and of course defenseless. There was nothing I could do to stop his words. He was older, and in the midst of these comments, people would burst out in laughter, and shake their heads in agreement.

My soul was wounded, and all I could do was sit and listen to the sound of my heart begin to come into agreement with the very words spoken over my life. I became curious about what it meant to be gay, what was butch, and lesbian. I had heard it so much that I believed every word. How can it not be truth, I mean everyone called me gay? My peers, teachers, other parents, now my own cousin. Everyone can't be lying about my identity, so since everyone believes I'm gay, I must be. So I thought.

Rejection, trauma, low self-esteem, and abandonment haunted me. It's as if these spirits came looking for me on a daily basis. From the moment my foot hit the floor, low self-esteem would say, "Good morning ugly. Good afternoon rejection, no one wants to be bothered with your bad self. Hello trauma, welcome to the world of torment." From the time I went to bed, abandonment screamed, "You're all alone." The more I grew, those words matured and walked with me daily, tormenting me and attempting to hinder my purpose. The more I was rejected, the more I turned to basketball. Basketball became my strong tower, and I ran to it for safety. This game was more than a game. In the twinkling of an eye, it seemed like it was becoming my God. I turned to basketball for comfort, security, and peace in my time of trouble. Whenever I felt any pain or hurt as a child, basketball was my outlet; it was my way of escape. The game became my mask in a time of trouble, and I put on the game to hide behind what I was feeling on the inside.

Things began to take a turn for the worse. Because my mother disapproved of me playing basketball, I now had to overcome the adversity of her desiring to take away the very medicine that cured my scars. I now had to sneak outside, and go through multiple obstacles to play the game I loved. Four houses down from me, a boy named Lupe had a basketball goal in his backyard, and that was the place of gathering. All the boys and even grown men from the neighborhood would gather in Lupe's backyard for tournaments.

I would show up dressed and ready with my T-shirt,

shorts, and Jordan gym shoes. I would have my hair gelled down in a ponytail, and would hoop it up from sun up to sundown. I couldn't just walk down the street to play because of fear of being caught by my mom, so I would jump gate after gate, ripping the skin off my leg from jumping fences and dodging dogs. By the time I got home, I needed a bandage to cover my wounds. I sacrificed my safety and was fearless when it came to playing the game I loved. I had the girly girls be on the lookout for my mom, and to report to me when she pulled up. If my mom asked for me, they knew not to tell her where I was.

The games would go on all night long. For hours, I was bumping into sweaty men, who played with their shirts off, backs dripping wet, and trust me they played me like I was one of the dudes. Playing with the boys sharpened my skills and I was ready to take the game to the next level. When Lupe wasn't available, I always had a plan B. We would go around the block on Shelley Lane, and run full court in the middle of the street. We would bring the rims in the middle of the street and take turns playing tournaments from Hilltop to Shelly. Whenever it got dark outside, we would bring out flashlights to finish the game because the streetlights weren't doing us any justice. We would be wrapping up the last game, and I could hear my mother on the other block screaming, "Moochie, it's time to get home". I refused to leave until the game was over. My heart would be beating, and everyone's mother would be calling for their kids to come home, but we continued to play until the game was over. If I won the game I trashed talked for a few minutes, punched my chest, high fived my teammates, and sprinted home. I would run through the front door, slamming the screen door, face dripped in sweat, white t-shirt dingy and dirty, and my hair all over my head. My appearance instantly sent my mother to red-zone. Dinnertime, the ball in my right hand while fixing my plate with my left hand. My mom would just shake her head, frown on her face, and say, "Go wash your hands and wipe your face."

Basketball was my comfort and had quickly become my best friend. Little did I know, that the same thing I looked to for comfort was the very weapon the enemy would use to abort and sabotage my destiny.

THE ENEMY HAS A PLAN TO

Homosexuality runs rapid in the basketball world for women. The spirit of homosexuality is difficult to dodge, whether you are participating or not, the seeds are launched because on every team there is at least one lesbian. Homosexuality and basketball for women are linked, they are coupled hand and hand. You witness gay coaches, masculinity, women intentionally desiring to turn out the girly girls, and so much more. You are surrounded by pride, and a lot of the girls playing basketball act masculine, and overcompensate to be something that they're not. I've heard people say just because you play basketball; you don't have to act like a dude. You find yourself trying to prove that you are better than a dude. See the enemy don't play fair, he takes every opportunity to open the door and launch his plan of destruction. "Age ain't nothing but a number" in my Aaliyah's voice. The enemy doesn't look at the fact that you are a child, he knows who you are before you do. The enemy knows your name, your identity, your destiny, and what God says about you. He is aware that before God wrapped you in flesh and sent you forth, that He had a plan for your life. So the enemy attempts to counteract this plan, by setting a plan to sabotage your destiny. Basketball in my eyes was all fun and games until the game began to cultivate my life and even my identity. Don't look at the ball and the game itself as if it's something bad; it's not. However, for me, the game was a demonic setup to destroy my God-given destiny.

Junior high school is when I discovered, desired and pursued to connect the dots to what I was feeling about women. While I was investing time and energy into creating an opportunity for me to prepare for my childhood dream of being a basketball star, the enemy was creating a plan for my life as well. When I look back on the timing of the enemy, it traces back to my youth when I was the most vulnerable. During that time, the enemy was working behind-the-scenes strategically to create my illegitimate identity. I grew up in a home with my mother who loved the Lord. She was a strong, God-fearing woman, but most of all, a praying mother. My father was in my life, and we had a very close relationship, however, he struggled with personal addictions that resulted in him being in and out of the home. When my father was present, it meant the world to me, and when he was absent, it cut me to the core. Not having my father around on a consistent basis left me unprotected, uncovered and rejected. The rejection of witnessing my father enter in and out of my life was traumatic. My mother was forced to provide the safety, security, and well-being of her three children. She worked extremely hard to provide and meet the needs of our family. My mother single-handedly carried the weight and responsibility of providing everything each of her children needed. As a child I witnessed my mother struggle and I always said to myself, I want to be the one to bless my mother the way she blessed me. I envisioned myself going to college and being the first on my father's side to graduate, and make it to the big leagues. I had a plan for my life at a tender age.

I fixed my gaze on pursuing basketball like never before. The Bible declares, have no other gods before me. I was treading on dangerous ground by allowing basketball to become my God. So with me having my full attention, my appetites and my desire fixated on the game, the enemy launched another missile, to ensure that I wasn't going anywhere. In sixth grade, I was exposed to the spirit of homosexuality by having a secret crush on my coach. Once the door opened to the spirit of homosexuality, the enemy had a field day. My life became the enemy's playground. So many issues stirred up and became more visible to me. Rejection, trauma, and abandonment rang loud in my ears. Whenever the demonic door of rejection, trauma, and abandonment opens, that child typically looks for it in the same sex, which opens the door to homosexuality and same-sex attraction. So the enemy was swinging doors open simultaneously in my life. I lacked the proper love and affection needed from my mother on a consistent basis because she was busy working, worrying, and doing everything possible to balance her personal issues, as well as trying to meet the needs of her children. So because I lacked the love and affection that I needed, I longed for it in another woman. I began to have crushes on older women teachers, parents, and coaches or any woman who affirmed me with her words and gave me their undivided attention. My father, on the other hand, was a good man, but his addictions had overtaken him, and as a result, he wasn't able to provide the level of supervision, protection and covering that I needed during the most vulnerable years of my life. While my mother was working to provide for the needs of her children, the post of my life was left unprotected, and I was not properly governed. Not being protected, resulted in the enemy having an opportunity to break in. When the enemy broke in and was granted access, every devil in hell shouted access granted!

The enemy declared war against my life and took advantage because I wasn't *shamared* (Hebrew for, *to be kept, or guarded*). The enemy released a demonic warrant for my arrest. The demonic police operated with strategy, patience, perseverance and endurance. The enemy seized it all and wasted no time in the realm of the spirit! He doesn't wait until you get older, he releases his attack and blueprint while you're still a youth. So the enemy crept in while my mother was working and my father was in prison, to release another attack. Because I was already exposed to same-sex attraction, it was the enemy's agenda to create a justified reason for me to hate all men. So the enemy used sexual abuse, absentee of a father, as my justification for living a homosexual lifestyle. The enemy is not satisfied with you being perverted, or simply just being gay, his plan is to create a new culture.

After experiencing sexual abuse, I learned to create my own measures of safety. The gates of protection around my life were not protected, so I created my own walls of safety. This agenda pushed me closer into the arms of a woman. The enemy doesn't play fair. He has a strategic plan in full detail on how to derail, disrupt, and abort your destiny. My appearance was beginning to change. I was becoming darker and darker. I lost my identity and began to hide behind the mask of pain. I felt a sense of abandonment and depression, so basketball became my blanket of protection. Basketball was no longer a game; it was my life and my livelihood. Whenever I felt pain in my heart, I turned to basketball. Whenever I felt any type of emotion, I took it out on the court. Many parents, teachers and family members called me bad, but they were unaware of the pain behind the mask. I was really aggressive, violent and angry. I took out my aggression on the court, and my aggressiveness was my outlet. I was expressing outwardly what I could not articulate inwardly. I was misunderstood, and I had no words to tell you how I felt so I did it outwardly while inwardly pleading, and crying for help. Anytime a woman patted me on the back, gave me praise or attempted to reach out to me; I became attracted to her. These behaviors followed me from junior high to high school. By the time I made it to high school, the stigma of me being gay tagged along. The older I became, the more immune I became to the stigma. Although I had never experienced being in a same-sex relationship before entering high school, I recognized early on that my heart and my appetite was fixated on women.

As I'm writing my story, I now understand why many young women feel they are born gay. They feel that because they were attracted to the same sex at an early age, often before puberty, that they were born this way. They are deceived by the enemy to believe this. Many people can trace back to as early as age six or seven years old, when they began experiencing same-sex attraction and gender identity issues. Let me share the revelation of the concept, "I was born this way."

Chapter 2
You're Not Born Gay!
Taking A Look At the Root of Homosexuality

" Behold, I was shapen in iniquity, and in sin did
my mother conceive me."
Psalm 51:5

*I*ve heard many people say, "I'm not changing, I was born this way! If God didn't want me to be gay, he wouldn't have given me these desires." I've also heard homosexuals say, "I been feeling this way since I was a child, I always had a desire for the same sex." Some of these concepts can lead one to believe that they were born gay. However, let's dive into a few of the root causes of homosexuality. First of all, I stand as a firm believer of the scripture, Psalm 51:5 which declares, "Behold, I was shapen in iniquity, and in sin did my mother conceive me." Yes, we were all shaped and born into sin. That scripture can't negate the very fact that although we were born into sin, doesn't mean God hasn't made a plan of escape. We were all born into something, but let's focus on the word that declares we can be born again through Christ

Jesus. We can parade around all day proclaiming, I was born this way, God made me this way, but that's not a justified reason to remain in that condition or state of mind. I'm reminded of Nicodemus in John 3:4-5 when he asked,

Nicodemus saith unto him, How can a man be born when he is old? can he enter the second time into his mother's womb, and be born? Jesus answered, Verily, verily, I say unto thee, Except a man be born of water and of the Spirit, he cannot enter into the kingdom of God.

Jesus clearly announced a new way, a new birth, and an opportunity to be washed, cleansed, purified, and made new through baptism, and confession of faith that Jesus Christ is Lord." Through the power of the blood, and the very fact that we can be born again, this breaks the power and strength of the myth I was born this way, therefore, I can't change. The life, death and resurrection of Jesus is vain to anyone who believes there is no other way, no new way, and no other option to be set free. Who the Son sets free is free indeed, and the time is arising for us to know the Son, and be set free from the deception of the enemy. You were born one way, but you can be born again through the admission, acceptance and baptism with water and spirit. We serve a Holy God. There is no way a pure, holy, righteous God could form unholy, and ungodly desires within us from which we could not be set free.

Many people get caught up in the idea of feeling like they were born a certain way because they can remember when they were a child and had certain desires for the same sex even though they were never exposed to homosexuality. What people fail to realize is that when they were in their mother's womb, the door was opened, and the enemy took advantage to launch his attack. The enemy doesn't play fair, so he began his operation in the womb. Therefore, God has already gone before the enemy to undo demonic attacks. God made a way of escape for us so we are without excuse that we were born a certain way. When we accept Christ as our personal savior, we are washed in the blood, cleansed of our sins, and become new creatures in Christ Jesus. We put away old things and everything becomes new. Becoming new and walking in righteousness overthrows darkness and our past is passed away. We now have the opportunity to walk in the purity and holiness of Christ through Christ. So if you feel that you were born gay, accept Christ as your personal Savior and allow him to purify you and make you new. Let's look at homosexuality and some of its roots.

Homosexuality is the outward manifestation (behaviors) of what's difficult for one to articulate, due to the spirit of rejection, trauma, and abandonment derived from a parental figure. While people are running around quoting, "God didn't make Adam and Steve, he made Adam and Eve," what should be addressed is that God didn't intend for single parenting to exist in the earth. The family is the heart of God, so we need to stabilize Adam and Eve. Children need both male and female, a mother and a father in their lives from the moment of conception. A daughter needs her father to Shamar her-guard, protect and cover her; to affirm, confirm, validate, love, and secure her in his love. A daughter needs her mother to nurture, love and praise her, and model womanhood. A man needs his father to affirm, confirm, validate, endorse, assure and protect him. He needs his father to teach him how to provide, love, protect and be a strong man. A son needs his mother to love, nurture, support and comfort him. When these elements and dimensions are missing, your child will seek what they need at an early age, and will begin to find idols to fill the void. If you want to fix the *Adam and Steve* situation, you must fix and stabilize *Adam and Eve*. God didn't leave Adam to be a single father over the earth, neither did he intend for Eve to be a single mother over the earth.

When there is a lack of affirmation, affection, love and nurture in the womb, the enemy enters before the baby is released into the earth. The enemy desires a spiritual genocide and your child is born with a death decree. Look at Moses before his very existence; Pharaoh issued death decrees to have the males murdered. The pharaoh of this day is already planning your child's death because he's aware that a prophet is in your womb. So he begins his demonic attack during the spermatic release of the seed that makes contact with your egg. So you're not born gay, you're just under arrest by the enemy, and his plan is to bring your soul into demonic detention, and ultimately hold a grip on you until you die so that you can spend eternity with him in the pits of hell. He has a plan to disrupt and abort your life by using rejection, trauma and forms of abandonment along with a host of other spirits to destroy your destiny. Your demonic launch party began in the womb for many of you, and just like me, this will open the door to perversion on a level you never imagined. So parents don't think for a second that your child woke up gay, or that this just happened. Some of this demonic activity was occurring in your womb.

Rejection, trauma, and abandonment don't begin when the child is older, some of those issues begin in the womb. Since this is my story, let's focus on what happened to me, and maybe my story will shine a light on your situation.

PRAYER
New Creatures

Let us pray this prayer that the power of deception will be broken right now in Jesus name.

I speak to the myth and deception that is declaring that you were born this way, and there is nothing you can do about it. I prophesy that the power of salvation will come upon you right now as you are reading this book. I declare that you will pause and think about the conversation Jesus had with Nicodemus so that He may have it with you. That you can be free, and that you have the power to enter the kingdom of heaven through baptism of water and the spirit. May your heart open with conviction, and your spirit begins to draw you to call upon the name of Jesus. I declare that the God, who answers by fire, will answer you right where you are. I declare every chain that entered at the gate of conception be broken in Jesus name. I strip Satan of his powers and com-

mand that he let you go right now in Jesus name. I break the power of his words that will rehearse that you can't be free, this is just the way you are, accept you or leave you. I break demonic words and whispers. I come against the lies of the enemy that there is no way of escape. I prophesy that you will drop to your knees right now and request that Jesus come into your life, come into your heart, and wash you in his blood.

I declare a tangible visitation to come upon you that will cause you to seek the father like never before. I declare that confusion is coming upon the enemy right now, and I plead the blood of Jesus and command demons of deception, rejection, trauma, abandonment, resentment, unforgiveness and bitterness to scatter. I command the strongholds of homosexuality and perversion to loose its grip, and prophesy by the end of this book, that you will embrace the truth, and that the truth will make you free. I call you a new creature even now, and declare that through Christ you have become new. The blood has the ability to do what we cannot do; the blood conquers, purifies, redeems makes us whole and breaks through the power of darkness. So Father in the name of Jesus, I release your arrows and winds to blow against every spirit released from the pits of hell to attack and torment your son and daughter. I release your love upon them right now that they will know that this battle is not theirs but yours, and if they accept you as Lord and Savior it is finished!!

Rejection

For me, the spirit of rejection began in my mother's womb. Once I became an adult, my mother informed me that she had attempted to abort me. My mother already had two children, had always wanted a girl and a boy, and since she had her son and daughter, she was satisfied and didn't want another baby. On top of that, she was going through a bad marriage with my father and was struggling financially. My mother can tell this version of the story better than I can. She attempted to take Humphrey 11 pills to abort me, however, the harder she tried to abort me, the stronger I grew in the womb. Due to my mother not wanting a child, during pregnancy, I was neglected of the proper love, nurture, and affection needed in the womb. The enemy forged his attack and allowed the seed of rejection to enter in, which was a door opener for the spirit of homosexuality.

"Rejection is dangerous, because when one is rejected he or she will self-reject, and walk in a fear of rejection."

Rejection began in the womb, and that spirit grew and matured the older I became. My father was in and out of prison, which further watered the seed of rejection. I was rejected by others due to my behavior and attitude and was considered the black sheep of the family because I was different. I was teased, talked about, and many didn't want to be bothered with me, so rejection grew. I began to self-reject and swallow the words of the enemy that no one wanted to deal with me. Once I swallowed the words, they digested within me which caused me to starve and long for acceptance, affirmation, approval and a desire to be wanted. I sought it out from anyone who would provide it. Because the seed of rejection was planted, it awaited the opportune time for someone to visit the garden of my mind, and water the seed until something sprouted. The mind is like a garden, it is filled with seeds both positive and negative, and can be planted within the mind of an individual. Once the seed of rejection was planted, it sat as seed in the garden, until someone came along to water it. When a seed is planted, and not watered, it dies, however, when a seed is watered, it gains momentum and strength which eventually manifests and sprouts. My garden was full of seed as a child and awaited the opportune time for flourishing.

In the womb I was turned down, my mother refused to accept that she was pregnant. I was denied the sufficient parental affection needed, so my appetite was fixated on whoever would accept and give me the very thing I longed for. Feeling unwanted begins in the womb, and the enemy's plan to remind that child that they should have been murdered, there is no reason for their existence is constant. When a baby feels unwanted in the womb, the fetus opens for the entrance of demonic rejection (Pigs in the Parlor). The enemy doesn't have a heart of compassion to wait on you to get older before he launches his attack. At the point of entrance, he comes in, invades and attempts to overtake. The enemy walked through the door, and held the door open for other opportunities in an attempt to abort my destiny. The enemy was angry that he was unable to abort me in the womb, so he attempted to abort my destiny. A failed abortion leaves the enemy with no other choice but to hunt down your destiny with a fierce desire to abort and murder your purpose. Hell is aware that you made it out and survived in the womb, so the enemy has the assignment to trouble you all of the days of your life.

Rejection is dangerous, because when one is rejected he or she will self-reject, and walk in a fear of rejection. Rejection is a stubborn spirit that wants to take your life and breath and hinder you from discovering the essence of who you really are. Rejection is a stronghold that grips you tight, and when you're used to being rejected, especially by parental figures, you look for it in someone else, and it's usually from the same sex.

Let's take a look at this scenario that traces back to when I was in third grade. When I was in third grade, I recall a cafeteria teacher taking the time to love me, nurture me, and show me affection. She was an older woman who was responsible for supervising the kids in the cafeteria and ensuring that we were well behaved. She would take the time to fix the burettes in my hair, pat me on the back, and smile and say, "I love you little Miss Sophia." This is when I began feeling something different about myself. In third grade, how can this be so? How can I be so young, and recall desiring such words from a woman my mother's age? What is this feeling? I was unsure of what I was feeling, so I bottled it up inside, and just enjoyed the sweetness of this woman. The words of this teacher watered the seed of my rejection, and so I began to long and look for someone to water me with their words of love and affection. Women by nature are affectionate and nurturers, so most of the women who complimented me, praised me, and spoke kindly to me, caused me to long and search for the words of a woman. I didn't have a label to put on what I felt; I just knew that the words of a woman were something I longed for. The enemy uses every open opportunity to pervert, twist and distort innocence to launch perversions. Rejection opened the door and because a woman watered the seed of my rejection- her tone, sound, and nature was tattooed on my mind, and I longed for exactly that, the words of a woman.

PRAYER

Father in the name of Jesus I come against the spirit of rejection that has opened the door to perversion, sexual immorality, and homosexuality. I command the spirit of rejection that entered at the point of conception to cause you to feel unwanted and unloved, to be bound. I bind the strongman of rejection that's holding you like a grip, causing you to self-reject out of fear of man. I rebuke anticipated rejection; that's operating through you and keeping you from godly relationships and pure covenant relationships. I bind demons of retaliation that keep you in a place of bitterness, resentment and unforgiveness, due to the lack of love and acceptance needed as a child. I command spirits of rejection to leave your heart, leave your mind, come out of your body, and let you go in Jesus' name. I release the fire of God upon rejection and command the spirit to lose its power, authority and grip off of your life. I break every negative word, negative thought, and negative experience that reminds you of your rejection. I break cycles of abuse in your mind, and speak to rejection declaring your time is up. You've lingered long enough on this soul, and I arrest you by the blood of Jesus. I come under the authority and declare at the name of Jesus you are terminated and arrested. No longer will rejection torment you, and no longer will it rob you of your joy, peace and ability to establish healthy relationships. I break generational curses of rejection, and every lie of the enemy that says you shouldn't have been born and that there is no need for your existence in the earth. I break the power of demonic words from family members and loved ones. I command rejection to lose its grip. I release the agape love of the Father to arrest every demon that entered through the womb and command this day that you are free. I prophesy that the truth of God's love will uncover the deceptions of the enemy. Be thou free today in Jesus name. I release acceptance, love, joy, peace and grace upon you and apply the blood in Jesus name.

TRAUMA AND ABANDONMENT

The enemy was furious that I had survived his death decree launched before I came out of my mother's womb. The enemy worked aggressively, putting in overtime to terrorize my childhood. He used multiple methods to bring an end to my destiny by looking for loopholes, and openings to creep in, and cancel the plans God had for my life. Not having my father in my life was traumatizing. Although my parents were married, my father was consistently in and out of my life, which resulted in my mother spending the majority of my childhood as a single parent. My father and I had a great relationship, we laughed, joked, and spent time together when he was present. He would be in my life for a length of time, then snatched away for years to spend time in prison. When he wasn't in prison, he had addictions that altered his ability to care for me. This went on for the majority of my childhood. The way we showed love and affection was through laughter, jokes and talking about one another. We weren't a hugging or affectionate family; we expressed love through criticism, which became a family activity. Although we would laugh, it opened the door for the enemy to use this time to water the spirit of rejection.

Every time my father would get arrested and spend time in jail, I would feel a sense of trauma and abandonment. My father wasn't present to protect, build me up, affirm me and love me the way I needed to be. Not having a father at the gates of my life opened the door for the enemy to come in and invade it. I experienced abuse, which resulted in me despising men. I felt unprotected and uncovered. The enemy doesn't play fair. He will seize every moment to make way for him to enter in, and engage war against your destiny. This trauma caused me to lack trust, faith, and security in a man. This further opened the door for homosexuality to be manifested, as I became more vulnerable and open to the voice and sound of a woman. My trauma separated me from the desires of a man and moved me into the arms of a woman. I was reminded daily by the enemy that my father wasn't there, he didn't care about me, his addictions came before his children, and these words were played like a radio set on repeat.

Being traumatized wounded my spirit, and once again the seed of trauma and abandonment were seeds added to the garden of my mind. Trauma and abandonment has the ability to affect one's speech. It causes you to stumble on your words, and it also leaves one with a stuttering problem, so, I acted out my feelings and emotions physically because I couldn't say a word about the trauma I endured. Trauma affects your ability to grow and mature, and it's the enemy's desire to keep you childlike, as you rehearse your pain over and over. When trauma and abandonment couples with rejection, it throws you into the arms of anyone who will love, accept, and embrace you. You become starved of affection, and because you're malnourished from the healthy love that you need, you go after anything that appears to be love. You thirst for affection and waddle around with your tongue out, craving a drink from someone's fountain of love. I know because I sought love, protection, affection, and words of security from a woman who made herself available.

PRAYER

Father in the name of Jesus I speak to the spirit of abandonment and trauma. I place the fire of God upon experiences of abandonment and trauma that traces back to childhood experiences. I come against the plans, plots, and schemes of the enemy that will leave you fearful and tormented from years of isolation, years of rejection, and years of a parental figure dropping the ball on your destiny. I destroy the yokes of bondage that have been sent from the pits of hell to terrorize you and cause you to look for security and safety in other places outside of God. I break every curse and negative word that says to you, you're unworthy, you're unwanted, and there is no need for your existence. I come against the spirit of abandonment that was sent against your youth to confuse you about your identity and rob you of your ability to love and trust those in authority.

I speak to the hurt, the pain, agony, and wounds of your heart that says to you, trust no man. I come against anger and rage from years of abandonment and people who you love walking out on you and turning their backs on you. I come against the devastation and pain of growing up without the proper love of a mother and a father. And I command spirits of torment to leave your mind and leave your heart in the name of Jesus. I break the spells of deception, false love and false security that will have you seeking comfort to fulfill voided places in your life. I pull you out of agreement with demonic dialogue that will tell you that because momma or daddy wasn't there, that surely God isn't in the midst to save or deliver you. I pull you out of the pain, and release the love of the father and declare unto you this day that Jehovah Gibbor(the God who defends) is your refuge, and will fight *every battle for you this day. I speak to trauma that comes from abandonment, isolation, and abuse. Trauma come out in Jesus name. I speak to the trauma that's attempting to rob you of your maturity, growth and ability to make proper and healthy decisions. I destroy the images of your trauma that have you rehearsing over and over who hurt you, and declare your release today. I speak to the mind and command the blood of Jesus to be applied, and declare that the blood covers every injury and every scene that's remembered of the day you were broken, bruised or abandoned. I speak to trauma and arrest you right now by the blood. I declare peace and release the power of God, the rescuing power over you right now. I come against every stuttering spirit and fear of opening your mouth, due to speech impediments caused by trauma.*

I command that this day you will open your mouth wide, and it shall be filled with the words of the Lord. I release the strong arm of God upon you, and declare restoration. I command every year the cankerworm, palmerworm and caterpillar have stolen from you is returned in Jesus name. I prophesy that the numbness of your heart that has been paralyzing for years due to the pain of abandonment and trauma, is destroyed by fire and this day your heart is awakened and flowing with the power and blood of Jesus. I release the manifestation of God's love upon you, and prophesy that your peace is returning to you, your childhood dreams are returning to you, and your security in the Father is returning to you right now in Jesus name.

CHAPTER 3
HOMOSEXUALITY & BASKETBALL
ON THE HIGH SCHOOL LEVEL

$\mathcal{I}$n 1995, the night before the first day of school, palms sweating, nose dripping wet, and heart beating with anticipation. High School would never be the same, or shall I say "Sophia Ruffin" would never be the same. I was ready to place my feet on new ground and leave my mark by making my name known. I intended to leave my mark by becoming a great basketball player and establishing a reputation once I left. My mind wasn't focused on meeting new people, and it definitely wasn't on getting an education, attending dances, or dating. My focus was on trying out for the basketball team, and beginning my journey towards college. I was a little afraid and intimidated about tryouts because this was the first year that two high schools in the area had come together to collaborate.

Although basketball tryouts were months away, I couldn't help but think about it. Every single night I would lay in bed, eyes wide open, staring at the ceiling with my ball clutched on the side of me, envisioning it all playing out. Sprints, suicide drills, crossovers, behind the back, running points, was all I envisioned. I thought about pushing point, and I could hear the crowds screaming my name. I had such an anticipation about playing basketball. My mind had no other focus; my attention span was on basketball, basketball, basketball. I didn't have time to focus on the excitement of being a freshman, I was already thinking ahead to my future, and who I would become in the days to come. As a teen whatever I put my mind to, I did it. I went all out with passion, because if I could see it, I could believe it. I would think about all of these things until I finally drifted off to sleep, dreaming about playing basketball professionally.

In the middle of my dream, ding, ding, ding. My mom would yell, "Moochie get up, it's time to get up." I was excited to get dressed and ready for my first day of school. My brother was a senior, and I assumed we would get on the bus together; however, he was already gone. I was so nervous. I got dressed and was ready to roll out. I creased & super starched my jeans, put on a t-shirt, some Jordan's, and stacked my hair. I wasn't able to make it to the shop to get my hair done, so I took some small curler irons, and tightly curled the short part of my hair, and curled the top. My hair had no bounce because I used to spritz it to keep it in place. Yuck....

I walked outside and ran into my neighbor as we walked to the bus stop together. She was tall, thin and very pretty. All the boys in the neighborhood found her to be attractive. She was my buddy because she knew all of my secrets, and even did a great job covering me when I was sneaking in

L's backyard to play basketball. I ran towards her screaming and obnoxiously, completely out of control, because I was so excited to step my foot on the high school premises. She had a breakfast sandwich in her hand and was nibbling on it. Every morning her father cooked breakfast and sent her off to school, encouraging her to have a good day. I often envied those moments, but would quickly put it behind me, and keep it moving. Tasha never ate her breakfast, so she would give me the breakfast sandwich once we were two houses past her home, and her dad wasn't watching us any longer. Her dad made a toasted sausage and egg sandwich with jelly. I smashed it and cracked jokes as we headed to the bus stop on 16th and Division.

Every morning we would witness drug dealers hanging out on the corner, and gangbangers standing outside yelling, "What up mooch!" I would yell back what up, trying to act like I was popular and familiar with so many people. When the bus arrived, I immediately walked all the way to the back and claimed my seat. For a freshman, I sure didn't act like it. Our bus was always loud and very rowdy. The bus driver would always threaten to kick me off because I was loud, disrespectful and out of control. Without hesitation, I had already made my presence and name known quickly.

Finally, we arrived at school and off the bus I go. Behind our bus were seven other buses full of kids in cliques; laughing, joking, and excited to head into the building. Some were walking with their heads down, with the look of confusion written across their faces. Immediately you could identify every freshman because they had a freshmen look about themselves. They had on new clothes and new shoes, and some of them had their backpacks full of school supplies, as they walked around looking like pure freshmen. You could point out the rookies quick, fast and in a hurry, they looked lost, and anxious all at the same time. I made sure I distinguished myself from the look of all the other freshmen. My brother was in his senior year, and I was excited to be in high school with him. I was very popular because he was like John the Baptist, he had announced my coming before I had even arrived. Walking through the hallway I was 5'6" about 130 pounds, yet my confidence added weight and dimension to me as I walked the senior hallway. People would scream out, "Hey, that's Lindsey's little sister." Immediately my name became known, because not only did my brother pave the way for me, but other relatives had already gone before to stigmatize my last name.

My family had made a reputation for our last name, and a stigma was attached that we were a bad influence; violent, disrespectful and failures. Nothing we began was ever completed, so my reputation preceded me. I had favor my freshman year because my locker was on the fourth floor, but my brother allowed me to use his locker, which was on the first floor. So while the freshmen were running back and forth from floor to floor, I was chilling with the upper classmen. I was the leader of my peer group, but when I hung around the older girls they always reminded me that I was nothing but a little freshman or fresh meat. I didn't hang out much with the freshmen girls because most of them only focused on the upperclassman boys. We would walk down the senior hall and all my friends would be giddy; blushing, laughing and acting very shy. They would point at the football and basketball players, as they whispered, "Ooh wee, he's cute, look at him, do you see him?" I would respond, "No, not really," in a nonchalant way. Uh, there goes that feeling again, what's wrong with me, why don't I feel like the other girls. I quickly suppressed my thoughts and kept it moving. I wasn't looking at the boys and didn't care if they were looking at me. All I was thinking about was basketball and having fun.

I'll never forget this day, August 1995, I was running fast up four flights of stairs for English class. Students were rushing inside the class trying to beat the bell as they grabbed their seats. The students were so prepared, they had books and notebooks, pencils, and even pens, they were ready to begin classes. I cruised in class just making the bell with a smirk on my face. I observed the class, and immediately walked all the way to the back, sitting in the last row, so I could look out the window whenever I got bored. Before I could make it to my seat good, I observed this teacher standing with her legs slightly crossed, long hair, glasses, dressed nice and looking very sophisticated, yet she had this look on her face that said, try me if you want to because I don't play. There was something about her that set me off, and I was up for the challenge. I knew that if I could get her in check early, I would be fine the remainder of the year.

As the teacher took attendance, she asked, "Sophia Ruffin are you here?" I sat quietly waiting for her to say my name again, just to stir up a situation. She says, "Sophia Ruffin," with her eyes gazing over her glasses. I hesitate then I raise my hand with pride and say here. She asks, " Didn't you hear me call your name the first time?" I said, "Yep, and I'm here," with a harsh tone. She then said, "Come here, come up here right now." She paused from the attendance sheet and started petitioning for me to come towards her. I said to myself, here we go. So I frowned my brows. My nose instantly began sweating, my heart raced, and I walked towards her. I got up from my desk aggressively, pushing the desk with the intent to make a scene so my peers would know I didn't play. Mrs. Love immediately stared me down and said, "Your seat is right up here smack dead next to me. Front row, right in my face, near me so that I can see you." I became so enraged that retaliation crossed my mind. Why is this teacher picking on me, what's the deal with her? She don't know me. I was ready to curse her clean out.

She then looked me eye-to-eye, face-to-face, like a mother disciplining her child, and said, "I know you, Ruffin, I've been there, and done it with you guys for a long time, but you young lady, it's something different about you. You have something special about yourself, and let me tell you this, you will graduate, you will go to college, and you will do something with your life, so sit up here right next to me." You would think that what she said would encourage me, but it triggered me. I felt judged and once again the stigma of my last name was affecting me. For the first time, I didn't feel rejected, she didn't put me out, she didn't get rid of me, but she took a stand for me, she took authority, and she spoke words of life to me.

Mrs. Love took a quick liking to me and within a week, she was my favorite teacher. I actually loved sitting in front with her because she would give me attention, love and affection. There was something very pure about this teacher, and I loved her with a pure heart and was impressed with her ability to handle me appropriately. She proved her commitment towards me, after going back-and-forth, round for round with me arguing and being disrespectful. The most powerful moment came when I realized that no matter how horrible I was in class, she never wrote me up or sent me to the dean. I witnessed her write other students up for saying or doing far less than what I was doing, but for some reason, she never wrote me up.

No matter how rude or disrespectful I was Mrs. Love took matters into her own hands. She dealt with me by getting back in my face and continuing to remind me that I was somebody special and telling me that I was going to graduate high school. My arms folded and eyebrows squinted, I looked her back in the eyes & for some reason I believed every word she spoke out of her mouth. Mrs. Love and I began to develop a very close relationship. She took me under her wings. She motivated me and pushed me out of my comfort zone, and she made me feel affirmed and validated. Finally, someone accepted my behavior without tossing me to the side like trash. I found myself excited to get to English class. I can even remember an assignment where we were required to write an essay on *Why the Caged Bird Sings*. I was very passionate and put forth a lot of effort in that assignment. I wanted to please my teacher, and I wanted to prove to her that she was making a difference in my life, whether or not I ever told her. I wanted my work ethic in her class to speak for itself. I actually got an A+ on that paper. Mrs. Love praised me, hugged me, and told me over and over that she was proud of me. Mrs. Love would even give me lunch money, and always looked out for her Sophia. She was the only teacher able to de-escalate me and keep me calm when I got into trouble with other teachers. She would push me, motivate me and inspire me to excel.

What I value most about her is that she took the time to get to know me and understand why I acted so badly. She showed genuine care for me as a person. I got in trouble in every other class. I had a social studies teacher Ms. Washington, and that woman literally made the hair on the back of my neck stand up. As soon as I walked into her class, she would kick me out before I could even take my seat. This teacher hated to see me coming, and as soon as I hit the door, she would say bye Ms. Ruffin. She never attempted to establish a relationship with me or get to know me; she just kicked me straight out of her class. I would run right up the stairs to the 4th floor, and complain to Mrs. Love, and she would calm me down quickly.

My behavior during my freshman year was out-of-control I limit tested, and felt like I had something to prove. I guess I was sort of bored because basketball season wasn't until October. Academically, I struggled and didn't apply myself in anyone's class other than Mrs. Love's. I never valued the importance of being a student-athlete, I focused on being an athlete and aborted the student version. In my mind I didn't need to prepare academically because I felt basketball would be my life, so why waste time taking tests, and putting in so much unnecessary time learning. I didn't prepare myself academically for the next level and I felt that my athletic ability would take me places my education could not. Although many advised me on the importance of an athlete conducting themselves appropriately on and off the court, I paid it no attention and continued to focus exclusively on the court.

BASKETBALL TIME

Finally, basketball tryouts were here, the moment I'd been waiting for. I was determined not to miss the bus, so I left class a tad bit early to get my stuff together. Today was the beginning of a new day for me, one of the greatest times of my life. I was excited and nervous at the same time, but I had to put my game face on. When I walked into the gym, I observed my surroundings and scoped out opponents and future teammates. I recognized a diverse group of young ladies. They were all different races, ages, heights and weights, but what stood out most, was the difference between girly girls and the more masculine women. I immediately thought to myself, wow, it's other girls here that look like Coach D, my sixth-grade coach. So, of course, I judged them, and took no time making my assessment, that oh she's gay, and she's straight. I sort of felt in between because I wasn't masculine outwardly, I was still on the fence about my identity. I was in a more curious state. I recognized how I was drawn to the more masculine upperclassmen because I desired to learn more about them, so I could figure out what was so weird about me.

There were a lot of girls in the gym. It was steaming with heat, and the smell of sweat and Bath and Body Works perfume burned my nose. The atmosphere was thick with adrenaline, competition, and even division because the col-laboration of schools was something new. I looked around and immediately my eyes were filled with the desire to be around the varsity players. I didn't want to even try out for the freshman team. I wanted to be with the seniors. I can remember newspaper reporters being present, interviewing and taking pictures of the varsity team, and speaking to two of the superstar seniors. I thought it was cool to sit back and watch the superstars in action because the entire time I kept repeating, soon Sophia it will be your turn. I was hoping for a Coach D, but I didn't realize that what I was really hoping for was a gay coach, I just knew I wanted someone I could relate too.

The funniest thing was the varsity coach was a very old white lady, who walked with a limp. She had a full head of white hair and OMG this lady didn't play. She was known as Coach Patty, and she was passionate about the game and had high expectations for the team. She took pride in winning and didn't have a problem disciplining the players. We began tryouts all in one gym to begin stretching as a team, and running a few laps, suicides and sprints before separating for the tryout. After conditioning together, the freshman and sophomores went to one gym to try out, while the varsity team had practice in the big gym. I felt confident about trying out for the freshman team, but my eyes were set on getting closer to the varsity team. I had this cocky attitude and felt like I got this, I didn't worry at all, I just knew I would make the team. I made the team and immediately I was placed on the sophomore team. I was excited because I was that much closer to being with varsity. I was so excited, I longed for and desired to be on the varsity team.

LOCKER ROOM & BUS CHRONICLES

During basketball season, you hear and learn a lot in the locker room and on the bus. The teams were not separated in the locker room, so as a 14-year-old freshman you are exposed to conversations that 18-year-olds are having. The conversations were detailed, drastic, x-rated and perverted. Most of the time when you were in a female locker room or on the bus with a bunch of female basketball players, it would sound like a bunch of men talking, because of the graphic nature and openness about women. The locker room chats were sexual. You learned about same-sex attraction, and the power of being turned out was more real than anything I'd ever seen before.

On the bus, the girls would laugh, joke and talk about

sex. Because I was a freshman on the sophomore team, I was on the same bus with the varsity players. The coaches sat all the way in the front of the bus so often they had no clue what we were talking about. Some of the girls would make fun of the girly girls, by making comments like you know you want to get down, you should just try it. Homosexuality was the center of our conversations. It was normal. There was no shame, no fears; it was normal. Locker room chats were something you couldn't dodge. No matter how hard you tried to ignore it you couldn't miss it. I was so curious I would always put myself in a situation to hear it because it gave so much clarity to what I was already feeling. Some of the girls already had girlfriends and were sexually active with other girls. You would learn about oral sex, and often hear statements like you don't have to worry about getting pregnant, and you should try it because a woman knows what another woman wants. Curiosity played upon my imagination and was beginning to overtake me. The seeds that were planted as a child were now being watered and waiting for manifestation. It was easy to determine who was gay, who was curious and who was straight.

Suddenly basketball and homosexuality were in the same bracket in my opinion. When we traveled from game to game, it appeared normal. It felt like if you were not gay, you were the minority. From the coaches down to the players, masculinity ran strong in the basketball arena. I found myself watching a lot of college basketball on television and observed the same common thread, that there's a link between homosexuality and basketball. Growing up many people who stigmatized women basketball players as gay, were focused on the ones who were more masculine. The girly girls didn't catch so much heat because masculinity was the face of women's basketball. My freshman year I still had some innocence and purity around my identity, however, the more I engaged in homosexual conversation, and the more I was around it, I began to get comfortable and badly desired to try it. Finally, I didn't feel all alone. I had an entire community of women who felt how I felt.

So, I quickly connected with people like me and was educated on how to be a stud. I learned the terminology so that I could identify my role, responsibility, and function. I wasn't just learning to be gay, and sexually active with a woman; I was being inducted into a lifestyle. Homosexuals have a language. They dialogue with one another using certain words. I remember admiring this upperclassman who was a superstar. She was masculine, she dressed like a dude, wore her hair like a dude, and was so chill, yet there was something about her that drew me. I would make every excuse to be in her presence. I wasn't attracted to her, but I knew she was in the life, I just knew it. Suddenly my appetite and fixations were set on discovering more about the life that was invading my imagination. I would often go home and think about the things I had learned in the locker room and on the bus.

I would open up the playground of my imagination and replay everything I had heard. At one point all I thought about was basketball, I would drift off and daydream about being a star player. But slowly my basketball goals were becoming secondary, and my new attraction and primary focus was homosexuality. I was caught up in the fantasy, and my mind was made up, if I was going to be a basketball player, I might as well be all in. I refused to fight all the desires I was craving, so my freshman year I researched and studied homosexuality, and looked for veterans to skill and train me in the life.

FRESHMEN YEAR

Freshman year was really difficult because I was learning so much about myself and my identity. I was searching for a way to justify what I was feeling. Often, I had to disguise my identity because my mother and my family wouldn't approve of the lifestyle to which I was ready to commit. So I just remained a little tomboy. I didn't go all out; I slowly manifested into the lifestyle of homosexuality by allowing it to begin in my mind first. My mother didn't come to any of my games my freshmen year. She didn't really approve of me playing, and she was often embarrassed by people's comments about me being butch.

Even though I was excited about being on the sophomore team, my mother didn't know much about it. I was playing really good, and thriving athletically. My god mom LaKenia was a huge support, she made it out to almost all of my games. She was a huge support and a huge fan. She would come and trust me the entire arena would know who she was- from the coaches to the players on the opposite team, and all the way down to the referees, they knew who she was because no matter what, all she yelled was three seconds in the lane. Basketball was going great. I was developing into a point guard and was getting better and better each game. While I didn't fully understand the role and function of a point guard, the older and more experienced I got, the more I began to understand. I though running point meant the ball was in my hands at all times, and I was to score, score, score, but I quickly learned that a point guard was more than just a shooter and that it carried a wide range of responsibilities, which I will discuss later in the book.

"With all this going on and being in the closet, I struggled. The struggles with my identity were beginning to play with my mind."

My freshman year I was exposed to more than just what it meant to run point, I was being impregnated with demonic seeds of homosexuality, and those seeds were sitting in my imagination waiting to be watered. I didn't feel ashamed or embarrassed to tell my teammates I had the desire to get down with a girl, however, I was afraid for anyone else outside my basketball circle to find out. Homosexuality was the norm for basketball players. It wasn't weird disgusting or even strange. My peer group at school would make comments about me being gay. I got offended and even got into fights because I was trying to convince them that I wasn't, and I would tell that I was just a tomboy. Whenever my mother questioned or became suspicious about my sexual preference, I would get offended, shut down and become angry because I felt like she was judging me. Although her gut instinct was right, I would still get defensive and angry. Because of this, basketball became a blank to hide my sexual preference from anybody outside of my covers. This caused a wedge between my mother and I because she knew her daughter was gay, she just didn't want to accept it, and on top of that, I denied it strongly. It was easy for me to play on my mother's emotions, and manipulate her by shutting down and making her feel bad for asking me questions. I wanted her to think that her discernment was off when in reality she was right. My mother recognized the shift in my demeanor, my attitude and even in the way I dressed. I didn't go all out, but I was beginning to change internally before the external manifestation took place. My heart, mind, body and soul lusted after basketball and women. All of these emotions and desires were bottled up with a lid on it, being filled, and awaiting the opportune time to explode. So I played it cool and told myself, just make it out of high school. Then I could live the life I desired with no limits, no boundaries, and no cares about anyone's opinion.

With all this going on and being in the closet, I struggled. The struggles with my identity were beginning to play with my mind. I couldn't focus on my grades. I was failing classes, getting into fights and getting suspended from school. I did just enough to get by. I was able to maintain my grades at a 2.0 average, which was necessary for me to play basketball.

My popularity began to grow because I was a freshman who had ended the basketball season on the varsity team. It was an amazing experience being around star players who were highly recruited for college. I was fascinated and desired to be the next star. I waited my turn and continued to develop my skills on the basketball court. The coach always praised me and told me to keep working hard and one day I would be next. I was sort of like a coach's pet, and I often was the one who gave it my all in practice- I came in early and left late. I hustled and did everything I needed to do to ensure my position in the future. I attended summer league games and was developing as a pretty good point guard. My freshman year my number was 24 because they did not have the number 23 available. I kept telling myself that when I got on the varsity team, I was going to be number 23 because I was like Jordan.

The summer before my sophomore year, I made plans to experience my first same-sex relationship. I became so curious about learning more about the lifestyle, that I sought out information. I heard about the party line through my peers at school, so I found myself dialing in and checking it out. After sitting in on a few calls, I decided to launch out into the deep by creating a name and testing the waters. Boy oh boy, I had no idea what I was opening myself up to, because the party line exposed me to homosexuality on a new level. I was asked to create a name, so I panicked, and the first thing I shouted was it's "Amari All." I saw my mother's Avon perfume sitting on the dresser called Amari, so I just used that as my name because I thought it had a swag to it. There were multiple options on the party line- men looking for women, men looking for men, and women looking for women. I didn't hesitate with the options because I knew exactly what I was looking for. The party line was an open call with multiple people talking in groups, so I listened to familiarize myself with the protocol before actually making myself known. The ages varied, from teenagers to full blown grown women. There were no boundaries, just everyone chatting in a group like one big conversational orgy. I was educated on three types of sexual preferences, and I immediately jotted down notes

#1.) Feminine Lesbian: Beneath the make-up, earrings, lipstick popping, blushed cheeks, tight jeans, high heels, matching purse, skirt, dress and all of the above that makes a woman, a woman, is a lesbian that is hidden. There is nothing noticeable that stands out to anyone that would make a person say, "She's gay." She's a glamor to look at, she's attractive to men, she smells good, she's kind-hearted, soft-spoken, gentle and meek. This woman doesn't just look for a butch woman; this woman will also date another feminine woman.

#2.) Butch Lesbian: The butch lesbian is better known as a "stud" She is more dominate, aggressive and masculine. The stud takes the lead role and functions as the male in the relationship. The stud is well-known and identified immediately by everyone as being a lesbian based on her dress, demeanor, and speech. This woman dresses masculine, has strong facial features, has either a low haircut, dreadlocks, braids, or hat on her head; wears sneakers, baggy clothes, and nowadays they sometimes wear skinny jeans. The butch typically is drawn to the feminine woman for a relationship, however, you will often see a butch with another butch. This woman shops in the men's section and is the aggressor sexually.

#3.) Bi-Sexual Lesbian: This woman goes both ways, and is attracted to both men and women. These women will date either sex depending on their preference at the time. A bi-sexual can be a feminine or butch woman, based on their sexual or relational desire.

Immediately, I knew that I wanted a feminine woman. In my opinion, it was disgusting for me to date a stud/butch woman when I was more of a stud. If I wanted to date a stud, I would have dated a man. But that's just my opinion. I was attracted to the feminine woman and desired to be the aggressor, the more masculine one. I didn't want to date a bi-sexual woman and didn't want to date anyone already gay. However, I had to learn to crawl in the lifestyle before walking. I had to get some experience under my belt, so I played around with the party line for a few months for practice. During the group conversations, everyone would be talking loudly and joking around. I heard so much; I felt like these people were living on another planet. I learned about sexual positions, toys, what to do, and what not to do in bed. My imagination was filled with desire and curiosity. I was anxious and nervous, but I knew I had to start from somewhere.

After sitting in on the group conversations, I decided to invite a woman into the private chat. She continued to say to me, you sound so young and so cute. I was flattered, and told her, yeah I'm in high school, and went on to talk about my basketball skills. She was very impressed and continued to compliment and stroke my ego. Her words were speaking my love language, so I stayed on the call with her for hours. Soon the conversations went deep, and she started asking me if I had ever gotten down. My heart paced, my mind raced, and I quickly responded, "oh yeah plenty of times." As the conversation was prepared to take another route towards phone sex, I heard the door slam and realized uh, my mom is home. I hung up the phone without saying bye, or anything. I was so embarrassed because I had lost my moment of learning something new.

Now my mind was made up! This summer would be the summer I would experience my first same-sex relationship. I mean, why not. I was already known as a butch, and was constantly being teased and called a dike, so why not be that person everyone assumed I was anyway. Since I wasn't able to drive to meet some of the people I was meeting on the party line, one of my friends on the team drove me around from place to place meeting some of these ladies. When I would go and meet some of these ladies, none of them were my type. They had some of the prettiest voices, but the ugliest faces. I'm sorry, that's just how I saw it back then. I would show up at their doors, and give them a fake name and say I'm at the wrong house. I would take off running in a full basketball sprint, to the car with my teammates, and scream, pull off pull off that lady was ugly.

One of my homies would say, that's what you get, meeting these ugly dikes off the party line. I would tell her to shut-up, and let her know that soon she would be doing the same thing, because she too was gay, but was still in the closet. We would all burst into laughter, and head south. So epic failure, no luck today, would be my thoughts. I would get home, and I would find myself back on the party line until I found the right type. After multiple failed attempts with the party line, I gave it a break, and said this stuff is crazy. Here it is, I was ready to get down, and I kept running into some monsters. Some of these women were my mother's age, and they knew I was 15 years old. I didn't care about the age, I thought it meant something to pull a grown woman, but it just wasn't my time.

I decided to spend the rest of the summer focused and in the gym. My high school hosted summer basketball games with different teams, so I was able to connect and establish friendships with a lot of other girls. We would exchange telephone numbers, and become friends even though we were opponents.

As the summer went on, I was told by my coach that I would be on the varsity team my sophomore year, but I would be the point guard coming off the bench. I was okay with that because I knew my junior and senior year would be my years to shine and flex.

Sophomore Year

Sophia, so keep it real, are you gay or what? These questions came from peers outside of my circle. I was upset each time someone outside my circle would question me. Why can't I just be a tomboy, why they in my business? So once again, I remained silent with my peers and kept it real raw and uncut with a few of my homies. Sophomore year I began to water the seed of homosexuality by seeking out a girlfriend. It was difficult because I didn't like the other girls on the basketball team, and I didn't really care for girls my age. My desire was growing stronger and stronger. My curiosity was reaching a high peak. I went back to the party line, where I was becoming bolder and bolder. I began to study, observe and analyze other women who would look like me.

One day a stud walked up to me and said I was turning into a stud. She was an older woman, and she gazed me in the eyes and said wow girl, you definitely growing into a stud. I asked why she said that because in my eyes I had not yet fully launched into the butch lifestyle. She said my mannerisms were stud like, and advised me that if I continued on this path, I would be a stud, and all the ladies would want me. This flattered me, and my ego enlarged itself. So I went on my quest of studying the role of a stud. I learned that studs were supposed to dominate, rule, control and play the masculine role. I was educated through party lines, and talked with other experienced studs. I learned the rules, roles, and functions of a stud.

Although I couldn't fully come out and be like some of the studs I saw, I took the time to invest, learn and discover my new life. I had to be patient because there was no way my mother would approve of me breaking out into the stud I desired to be. I waited for my time and my coming out party. I didn't fully look like a stud, but I began to take on the personality. Internally I was watering and transforming my identity in preparation to break out when I departed for college. I was already transformed internally so by the time I went to college the only thing I had to do was put on the garments outwardly to express who I had already become. I already knew that I wasn't attracted to other studs. However, they were my homies. I was attracted to the girly girls. I spent endless hours watering the seed of perversion and homosexuality by anxiously awaiting my opportunity to act out what I imagined.

I starved for conversations about homosexuality and wanted to learn everything I needed to know. I quickly learned the culture, dialogue and language of a stud. I knew that since I was a stud, I needed to date a feminine girl. I wasn't attracted to studs, or anyone who acted in a tomboy-ish way. I wasn't attracted to women who were lesbian or bi-sexual, I wanted to convert, and be the one who would turn a woman out. Many may ask me why, why did I want to turn someone out. It was this challenge, this power, and control I desired, and I wanted to see if I really had the in-fluence to get someone to alter their way of thinking for me. Homosexuality wasn't about the sex for me. I learned early in my desire to be homosexual that it was about power, control, and conversion. So I was on pause before I could fully operate, and my time of public revealing had not yet come. I couldn't fully operate at this point in my life because I was still in the closet. I couldn't totally walk out this lifestyle to the full capacity, because of the pressure of my mother being disappointed and fear of what others would think. I began strategically making my plans and knew that as soon as I broke out, I would be on a mission. I couldn't wait to be me, without the fears or worries of anyone in my family having a say so over how I dressed, and how I behaved.

Whenever anyone questioned my sexuality, it was easy to hide behind basketball, and just say, I was a tomboy. I was able to fake it until I made it. The only one I was fooling was myself, and I hated it, but in due time, I kept encouraging myself that I would be free. Freshmen year it was seedtime, sophomore year was watering time, now as I approached my junior year, this was manifestation time. I want you to know that homosexuality doesn't just break out in one day. One doesn't wake up and declare, good morning family; I'm gay. These seeds have been planted from the beginning and have been lying in the garden of the mind awaiting watering with the purpose of future manifestation.

JUNIOR YEAR

Junior year it was manifestation time. I was the starting point guard, and my popularity began to spread like wildfire. I used my popularity to get whatever I wanted and enjoyed this new season of my life. I developed a strong sense of cockiness and often found myself frustrated because inwardly I was a full mature stud, but outwardly I couldn't yet reveal myself! The party line increased, and I was well known on the call. My name quickly switched from Amari to Thug Passion. I was playing basketball, falling deeper in love with the game, and falling deeper in love with the lifestyle! I was exposed to homosexuality and basketball like never before. I became one of the premiere leaders of exposing homosexuality to my peers and introducing them to the life by sharing the party line with them, and discussing some of the wisdom I had learned from others. I no longer had to search out women; women were beginning to search for me. My name was becoming known in the community. I was in the newspaper, and I was rising on the court as well.

The summer of my junior year, I played on a summer league team for Cedar High School. During this time, I had developed friendships with other studs, and when we hung out, our conversation was like high school boys waiting to take the virginity of a female. In the locker room, it was the norm to chat about one of the straight girl's body parts, as she showered or undressed. The straight girls would laugh it off, and say stuff like stop playing. However, no boundaries were established. The locker room was free for all, and no one got offended.

It was the norm to cross boundaries, smack someone on their butt, or make a comment about their body. The locker room was Satan's playground to begin planting seeds in the mind of anyone listening and receiving. Some of the straight girls took it as a compliment, and would smile and brush it off, however, the true intent was to plant the seed of curiosity, which would ultimately cause her to consider trying it. As the saying goes, curiosity kills the cat, and the plan was to make one so curious that they would just give in. The pressure that's in your face day in and day out during basketball season is no joke. No one was safe, and the older I became, the wiser I grew regarding my ability to convert and turn someone out. I didn't want to date anyone on the team, so the majority of my time was spent joking and planting seeds in their imagination, making them pregnant with my words so that they would one day give birth to them by engaging in a same-sex relationship.

While on the party line, I met multiple women and spent the summer of my junior year getting into all type of chaos. I had this really cute voice, and I wasn't fully masculine. However, I had tomboy tendencies, and many of the women on the call were attracted to that. I met women off the party line. Some were epic failures. However, I enjoyed meeting new women and was using this time to practice and develop my skills as a stud before going off to college. I met some women who were much older than me, and I found myself attracted to them. This lifestyle suddenly became a game, a challenge, and I enjoyed every moment of it. I took the steps of launching out on the party line and built a reputation for being a young "stud". At this point, I was really distracted because the only thing I thought about was basketball and women.

Basketball and homosexuality walked hand in hand. Being on the basketball team, and thinking you are going to dodge the spirit of homosexuality is like standing in the middle of the highway and not believing you will get hit. You can dodge traffic for a while, however, the longer you stand in the middle of the highway, the potential of you getting hit is extremely high. That's how it is for women and basketball. You play the game long enough, and escalate higher and higher; you are likely to experience a same-sex relationship. My junior year I began to change and was becoming darker and darker in my thoughts. I wasn't interested in dating any of the girls on the team, so I sought out my relationships by using the party line. Opportunities were opening for me, and some of the girls at school were seeking me out and wanting to experiment sexually with me. They wanted to keep it a secret and didn't want anyone to know, so the day came when I became sexually active with multiple school-age peers. Due to me dating feminine girls, it was easy to hide, because I would just tell my mom they were my friends, and on top of that, these girls didn't look gay at all. The summer of my junior year launched me into full manifestation. I was turning girls out left and right. I never intended on having a relationship with these girls. I felt like one of the guys, just hit it and quit it. I was moving off adrenaline, and the more sexually active I was, the more prideful I became.

The school year began, and the pressure was on. It was time for me to take my academics more seriously because this was the year I would take my ACT and SAT. My grades were declining, and I was only performing at a level necessary to keep me on the team. I couldn't focus on anything because my thoughts were full of the words of the last woman I spoke with before school, and on what college I would attend. No matter how many people advised me on the importance of being a student-athlete, I failed to heed their advice and continued to work beneath my capabilities. I didn't put in the additional work academically, and I did just enough to get by. My mind was going 24 hours a day. I woke up with women on my mind and went to bed with women on my mind. I stayed full off the conversation of any woman who took the time to tell me good morning, and tell me goodnight. My peers were accepting of my sexuality, so I began proudly sharing with others that I was gay. I had already been exposed sexually with girls, so I didn't mind anyone who asked. I would hear some of the girls laughing and making negative comments, but I didn't care because the main ones laughing and pointing were the main ones asking if could I spend the night at their houses. So I just laughed, brushed it off and kept it moving.

Basketball season was in motion, and I was ecstatic. I didn't worry about trying out; I was already one of the captains on the team. I spent my junior year really focusing on basketball and developing my skills as a point guard because I was getting closer to my dreams coming true. As the season began, the expectations were high, and I was looking forward to kicking off the season. Tryouts were fun, although I was already on the team, I enjoyed watching the freshman panic and worry if they had made the team or not. They were so cute. They were nervous, anxious, and looked up to me as an upperclassman. These freshmen looked at me, and it reminded me of the days I was in their shoes. I made them feel comfortable by praising them, encouraging them to go hard, do their best, give their all, leave it all on the floor. I was honored to be their role model, so I worked hard and gave them something to look up to.

My junior year my eyes were opened wider to homosexuality and basketball increased. As I traveled to different games and played against different schools, I witnessed so much boldness with girls kissing their girlfriends in the stands. Girls holding hands with other girls, it was out there, and for some reason, I was extremely shocked because although I was in the lifestyle, I wasn't out in the open. I couldn't imagine kissing a girl in front of a crowd of people, especially other adults. It was becoming more normal than a male and female relationship. I enjoyed playing certain schools in our conference because I would see a lot of girls who reminded me of me. Studs were everywhere.

I was trying to focus on the game, but at times, it was difficult to focus with so much distraction staring you in the face. We would go to away games, and it wasn't uncommon for a woman to attempt to talk to me while I was sitting in the bleachers watching the sophomore game. I found it flattering, but I didn't want to lose focus on the game, so I just allowed them to flirt with me while I thought to myself, it's game time, show off time. I felt like I had my own fans in the crowd, but I didn't allow it to affect my flow. As the season was getting under way, I felt like I was missing something. I knew exactly what I needed this season, and that was my mother at the games.

So much was beginning to happen for me athletically, and I really wanted my mother to be a part of what was taking place. Although my godmother attended every game, I wanted my mother there. I wrote my feelings out on a sheet of paper, and asked my mother to sit down, so I could express my feelings. I begged my sister Alison to be present because I was ready to go all out sharing my emotions. I wanted my mother to know that I needed her presence at the games. After sharing my heart with my mom, she didn't just listen to me, she responded to my needs. It took one conversation, and my mother's heart was moved. She agreed to come to the games and support me. She became my number one fan overnight. I was sort of nervous about her coming to the games because I feared one of my peers would slip up and say something about me being gay.

My mother and my Uncle Lorenzo came to every game, home and away. My uncle and I were close because he stepped in and filled the voids I had in my life. He collected newspaper clips, and helped me develop a scrapbook, and he purchased me and my teammate's dinner when we won games. He was a great all-around support, and it was awesome having him and my mom at the games. My junior year was special because my family was on board, I was the starting point guard, and I had one more year before graduating and heading off to college.

Junior year went well, although I had a lot of distractions with the spirit of homosexuality, I was developing as a solid point guard. I didn't fully understand the role of a point guard until college, so I'll wait to discuss that role later in the book.

SENIOR YEAR

OMG, senior year, it's here. My time has come. I was excited and couldn't wait to graduate. Freedom, freedom, freedom. My academic performance was not so great, and my grades were not where they needed to be. I didn't focus on the ACT and I definitely didn't focus in class. I spent a lot of my time playing around and giving my time and attention to playing basketball. I was nervous because I wasn't sure what my future held, but it sure was my desire to get out of Chicago Heights. I was ready to become that person that was bottled up on the inside and ready to express everything I'd been holding on to for years. I couldn't wait to get away just to be myself.

All I could think about was freedom, freedom, freedom. Freedom from the opinion of my family, freedom from the opinion of others, and definitely freedom to just be Sophia. I had a lot of pressure at this point because most of the girls in my area were already signing their national letters of intent and I choosing their colleges, and here I was busted and disgusted. I wasted so much of my time focusing on amusing my flesh and seeking girls, that I totally missed out on advancing academically and preparing for this moment. I thought to myself, Sophia your entire life has been built around adversity, so this is just a loophole. One thing about me, whenever I faced adversity I never quit, I always bounce back. I've been a comeback kid since birth. Adversity didn't detour me from striving and advancing. My senior year I had to make some adjustments, and figure out a plan. I knew one thing to be true; I was leaving Chicago Heights.

My senior year I was beginning to build a better reputation with the teachers and staff based on how well I was able to maintain three years of high school without dropping out or getting into too much trouble. I was beginning to develop a positive reputation and was beginning to focus academically with hopes that I could get into someone's college. Every now and then I would go to the fourth floor to visit Mrs. Love. When I did run into trouble for maybe getting smart with a teacher or being disrespectful, Mrs. Love still put me in check, jacked me up, and reminded me that this was my senior year, and I needed to do better.

Mrs. Love continued to mentor me even in my senior year. I was the French Club president my junior and senior Year. I wasn't fluent in French and didn't know much. However, my peers had voted me to be the president both years. I was proud and honored to be the president, so I paraded around school announcing it to anyone who would listen to me. Both years I was also the lead salesperson with Bom Bom's (those fruity candies), because I had raised so much money, I would be allowed to go to Paris for the senior trip. I was working hard, hustling them packs like a drug dealer selling nickel bags on the block. I was making money for my trip. Senior year came and it was time for me to see how much money I had raised. The teacher Ms. T, who was old Caucasian woman, 4'9", 160 pounds, wore glasses, had spiked grey hair. She looked me straight in the eye and stated, "Sophia, unfortunately, I don't think we can trust taking you overseas honey because your behavior hasn't been consistent, and we can barely trust you in America." You're talking about furious! My home girl Shante laughed uncontrollably with tears running down her eyes. I kicked over a few desks and stormed out of her room. I ran four floors to find Mrs. Love, and she deescalated me in five seconds. She didn't allow me to lose it, although I was steaming, and smoke was coming out my nose. I was ready to knock Ms. T's head off. She knew from day one I wasn't able to go, but she wanted me to sell them bom bom's. When I look back at that moment, I crack up. Wow, who manages to get awarded president two years in a row, but can't make the trip to France—only Sophia Ruffin.

I began to recognize some serious changes in my personality. My desires and my appetite kept growing. I was the leader of the team, and many of the freshman and sophomores looked up to me. I wasn't into any of the freshman or sophomores. However, I was honored that they looked up to me and admired me. I sort of felt like a big sister to some of the kiddos. We still cracked jokes in the locker room and talked about our girlfriends on the bus, but most of the time I made the freshman sit in the front of the bus, so they weren't exposed to some of the conversations that we were having. At this point, I had already experienced same-sex relationships and was engaging sexually. Although I still wasn't out of the closet, my girlfriend understood that I couldn't fully operate as a stud because I lived with my mom. It was eating me up inside because I really wanted to break out and be dominant, but I held on a little while longer.

Basketball season went well. I was a great point guard. I made the all-area for the Chicago Tribune. I was in the newspaper, and was player of the week a few times, and honorable mention All-State. My team made it to the second round of regionals, and we lost to one of the number one teams. Because I was always in the newspaper and wanted to keep up with my clips, every Sunday I would sneak outside and steal my neighbor's paper. I would take out the sports section and set the paper back on his porch. I did this the entire basketball season, thinking he had no idea I was stealing the sports section, however, a few years later Mr. Jones smiled and said, "Sophia I knew all along, but I wanted you to keep your clippings." I was so embarrassed, but I thought it was funny. My neighbors and family, they all believed at this point that I was going to make it to the WNBA because that's all I talked about. They supported my dream and believed with me.

The season was over, and I had not yet figured out what college I was going to attend. I wasn't getting many offers due to my grades and my ACT score. I struggled academically and only did enough to get by. I never heeded the advice of my guidance counselor regarding being a student-athlete, and how important my GPA was on the collegiate level. I was too busy chasing my dream and girls. I was so stressed out, but I couldn't faint, I had to rise up. I quickly accepted the fact that I wasn't going to a D-1 university, so I began to establish goals around going to a D-2 or junior college. I wasn't defeated; I still had a chance to make it to the league. I was destined to make it, I mean this is what I built my life around—girls, sex and basketball. I created my whole identity around being a WNBA player and I barely knew what I wanted to major in, because my whole focus was on being a WNBA player. I just knew that I would be the one that would buy my mama a house, pack her up and get her out of the hood. I saw myself traveling all over the world to play basketball.

I imagined Dick Vitale announcing my name, and I heard the commentators announce at guard, a 5'6" rookie from Chicago Heights, Illinois, Sophia Ruffin, number 23. I could hear it. The words were so real as if they were audible. I saw myself with multiple women surrounding me, and I was living the life of a stud, finally living the life I envisioned. No roadblocks were in the way, but it was all good. I was determined to make it because surely this was the will of God for my life. I began to pray and remind God. I prayed with the team before every game. I prayed the sports prayer out of the book my youth pastor's provided me. I was reminding God of the words He never said, but I pursued my destiny with a passion. Basketball season came to an end, and it was time to decide what lie ahead. I was afraid, nervous and anxious. I ended the year as the team's MVP, yet I didn't know what the future held for me.

CHAPTER 4
THE POWER OF THE SPOKEN WORD

"The tongue has the power of life and death, and those
who love it will eat its fruit."
Proverbs 18:21

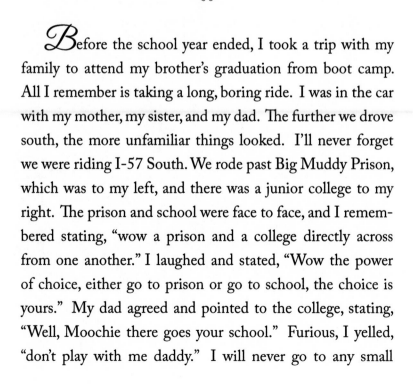

$\mathcal{B}$efore the school year ended, I took a trip with my family to attend my brother's graduation from boot camp. All I remember is taking a long, boring ride. I was in the car with my mother, my sister, and my dad. The further we drove south, the more unfamiliar things looked. I'll never forget we were riding I-57 South. We rode past Big Muddy Prison, which was to my left, and there was a junior college to my right. The prison and school were face to face, and I remembered stating, "wow a prison and a college directly across from one another." I laughed and stated, "Wow the power of choice, either go to prison or go to school, the choice is yours." My dad agreed and pointed to the college, stating, "Well, Moochie there goes your school." Furious, I yelled, "don't play with me daddy." I will never go to any small school in the back of the desert. I'm not going to any junior college looking like this." My dad continued to tease me, and state over and over there goes your school. If you know my dad, he will run a joke into the ground, so he kept on saying, "There you go, there is your school baby girl." With pride I fully expressed, I'm too good to end up at some junior college in this country bunk area, especially in the middle of nowhere. This stupid. My dad laughed and laughed. On our way back from my brother's graduation, my dad stated again, "There you go Moochie," I brushed it off, and put that thought away because I knew I wasn't going to end up at some small school in the middle of nowhere. Please, not me. My dad always had a way of encouraging me and making light of a negative situation, and to be honest, his words were speaking life, and he didn't even know it.

I went on a few college visits with my coach, who provided me transportation to a few schools. Each school we visited, I didn't fit in, or I felt like it wasn't the right school for me. I was becoming discouraged because graduation was slowly approaching and everyone kept asking me what school I was going to. I was sick and tired of saying I don't know. I was sinking into a depression because my dream was fading away. There were a few junior colleges in Chicago I could have attended but there was no way I was going to stay in the area, I needed to get away from home so I could finally let the top off this bottle I was hiding. I wanted to release the inner enemy that had been hibernating for years waiting to be released. One particular evening around 9:00 p.m., I was at home in my room laying across the bed wondering what about my next plan. The phone rang, and I answered with a slight attitude. This man with a country accent and very excited tone asked for Sophia Ruffin. I responded, "Who dis?" He responded, my name is Coach Wells. I'm the women's basketball assistant coach for Open Lake College in Southern Illinois. I asked him how he had gotten my number, and proceeded to tell me that he had heard about me, and wanted to know if I would be interested in visiting. I was a little resistant. However, I didn't have many options, so I responded, sure. I got his information, contacted Coach Patty, and we set a date for me to do a visit. I ran into the kitchen and told my mom; she was relieved and agreed to take the trip. My mom was very encouraging and supportive. She was starting to believe in my dream. We called my coach, and she agreed to transport us for a visit. I shared with my friends that I would be going on a school visit and that I was leaving Chicago. I didn't care what school I went to at this point; I just didn't want to attend any junior colleges in Chicago. I was longing to get away from home, so I could be free to be me.

My mom and I prepared for the weekend trip to Open Lake College. We were packed and ready to go. My coach arrived, and we traveled over 3 hours south to our destination. When we arrived at the school for the visit, it was a total culture shock. As we drove closer to the campus, it was surrounded by tall bushes, gravel rocks, deer and crazy bugs flying in my face. I was completely shocked as we passed several farm sites with pigs and cows. I was thinking to myself, what the heck is this. When we arrived and got out the car, I was so disappointed, because I didn't see not one black person, and I definitely didn't see anyone who looked like me. I began to worry about me being a gay, black girl in an all-white community. As I made it inside, the coach greeted me with a handshake and a smile.

Another shocker because I was used to gay, female coaches, and suddenly I was dealing with two married men, who were coaches. Bummer, what is this? I looked into the sky and felt like this was a curse. When I walked in and saw the gym, it was huge compared to high school, and the colors were red and white, which were my favorite colors, and the gym floor looked amazing. I saw a few white girls shooting hoops, and I thought to myself, they suck. They were shooting organized shots, free throws and working on ball handling. I thought to myself, well if I do attend this school at least I can be the superstar because these girls suck. I toured the school, and my mom and I talked with the coach. My mom appeared to be happy that her daughter was on a college visit, and seemed excited that her baby was being offered a full ride scholarship. I was the first person in my family on my father's side to go to college, and my mother was proud that I was going to get a scholarship and ultimately play the game that I loved. My mother had begun to like basketball, and she had quickly become a fan of mine.

The coach gave me a tour of the school and took me to the locker room, as well as the fitness center. He talked to me about the school, his expectations and my opportunity to grow in the point guard position. He also talked to me about how coming to a junior college would be good because I would have the opportunity to attend a Division I or Division II school after two years, so I was excited. I felt like I was still on track to make it to the WNBA. Adversity always seemed to push me, motivate me and inspire me, so once I swallowed the fact that I could not go directly to a Division I school, I decided I was going to use this opportunity to overcome adversity. As long I had a basketball in my hand, and was able to dribble the rock, I was okay.

After touring and talking with the coach, I spent some time playing basketball, working out, scrimmaging and running point with the team. I felt out of place because I was the only stud. These girls weren't gay; they were all dating baseball players. I decided to focus on basketball and worry about my sexuality later. We stretched, and I put on my Nike shorts, Jordan's, headband and wristband. Of course, I had the whole point guard outfit. I put on a tank top, so my muscles could show, but to be honest, I was on the chunkier side compared to these girls. I felt like I was in control. I ran the point; I set the pace, and I felt like it was my time and my opportunity to prepare for the next level. The longer I stayed and visited, the more comfortable I felt. I decided that attending a junior college in southern Illinois was a good choice for me, so I took the test for admission and decided that this would be my school of choice. The greatest part about attending a junior college was that I would be staying in my own apartment off-campus with a roommate.

I was excited to be able to have my own place because now I could finally be me. Sophia can break out, and all that was locked up on the inside of me was anxious to be revealed. I just didn't know what would happen because I didn't see any girls who were like me. I was a little afraid, but I knew that once I came on the scene I would be able to convert others, whether they were black or white.

Later that night, after spending the day on campus, the coach picked me up and gave me a tour of the closest major city, Mount Vernon, which was about 15 miles from the college. I didn't see any African-Americans, but I just rolled with the punches and said I was going to come and do two years here before transitioning to a university. The coach continued to drive through the town, as he pointed out the downtown area. I asked, "Coach where at?" He said, "This is it." I was in a state of disbelief, how could ten small buildings, a courthouse, and a few stores possibly be downtown. I asked about the mall, and he took me to a parking lot that had a few stores, and none of them were my type of stores. I was shocked, what is this place?

I was excited about returning to Chicago and letting everyone know that I'd decided on a school, and I was signing my letter of intent to attend junior college. Being 3. 5 hours away from home was perfect, I had enough distance and space to live my life. My peers were excited for me, and I was stress-free, so I decided it was time to kick it for the summer. The weight of deciding on school was over, so I could spend time focusing on girls.

Now that the wait was over, I was looking forward to what was coming next. Not that I was surprised, but my parent's separated after 26 years of marriage. What a crucial season to separate. Senior year, college in the future, graduation and now this. Really, I didn't sweat it. During this time, me and my mother's relationship began to grow. Although she never asked me about my sexuality, I could tell she was beginning to know, but we didn't talk about it much.

My mom really wanted me to go to prom because it was my senior year, and she wanted me to dress up like a girly girl. So I decided to go to prom with one of my friends who was a very nice guy. I allowed my mom to get me dressed for prom, and I decided to go all the way out and be a girly girl. If it was up to me I would have rocked a tux and took my girlfriend, instead of totally being something that I wasn't. I was in a relationship at the time, and I had to explain to my girlfriend that I was going to prom, and I was going to be a girly girl. She decided to stay home and didn't want any part in witnessing me look like a girly girl. Heck, I didn't want anyone seeing me girly, especially not her, so I begged her to stay at home because I felt embarrassed.

My mom had a great time shopping and taking me to multiple boutiques to look for a dress. We were on a dress hunt, and she finally found one that was perfect. We checked the tags and this dress was four-hundred bucks. She was determined to get me all dolled up. She bought me some heels, got my hair, professional makeup and nails done. I mean my mom went all out for prom. I hated the entire process, but I did it for her, just for her, I tell you. I mean everyone at school laughed, and kept saying they couldn't wait to see Ruffin in a dress. My mom had a limo escort us to prom. All of her friends and our family came over to take pictures and see me off. Everyone was cheering me on. Neighbors came out to on their porches and my brother's friends were riding by screaming, "Look at Moochie." I broke out in a hot sweat from all the attention. I was so uncomfortable and couldn't wait for this moment to end. I was already doing a countdown on it ending before it began. The entire prom dress and the whole girly girl thing messed up my perception regarding other girls. Usually, I would desire to hit on a chick, but as long as I was all made up like a girl, my eyes didn't even look at them in a sexual manner. I was wondering what was going wrong, so I knew this was a mistake. This girly girl look was messing with my lifestyle, and all of a sudden, for a quick second, I didn't feel gay. I didn't understand, what was happening. All I knew is that I needed to get this prom over with so that things could get back to being normal.

My date complimented me. He thought I looked nice, but that was it. I said to myself, the minute we take these pictures, we are leaving prom and going downtown to hang out! We made it to the restaurant for prom and the teachers and my peers were screaming, whistling and shocked to see me dressed like a girl. They all kept saying, " Oh Sophia you look so cute, you should dress girly more often." I wasn't trying to hear a thing. I was only focused on getting out of this stuff. After prom, we went downtown for dinner and drove around. While in the limo heading home, I popped off my nails. They were hurting so bad, because they were acrylic, and you can't just pull them off. I was so determined, I was just snatching them nails off one by one, pulling skin, hang-nails bleeding and all, but I didn't care. When I came back home, as soon as I walked in the door, my mother asked, " What happened to you." I had already started messing with my hair, attempting to wipe off the makeup, heels in my hand, and had a hand full of broken nails. My mom responded, "You wasted all of my money. You could've left those nails on a few days longer." I mumbled under my breath, "You had your moment, and you will get your picture. It is finished."

Meanwhile...It's Almost that Time, Graduation!

My mother threw me a graduation party, and I got so many gifts, and so many people blessed me before I left for school. I received all the things I needed to prepare me for college and had all the essentials I needed to graduate. The time arrived, graduation was here, and I graduated. The next chapter of my life was ready to begin. High school days were finally over. I survived, and I made it out. I didn't accomplish the goals I desired in the exact order I planned. However, I was moving towards accomplishing my dreams. Everything was working in my favor even in the midst of adversity. I was destined to break out, and be the stud that I desired, practiced and prepared for. I spent my high school years preparing for college; now it was time for college to prepare me for the NBA.

Who would have ever thought that my father was prophesying, when he declared that I was going to Open Lake College. That was a practical joke but in my world, it was the power of the spoken word, something in which my entire life has been shaped and molded.

CHAPTER 5
JUNIOR COLLEGE

$\mathcal{F}$inally, I can breathe. My mom and her friend dropped me off and got me all settled in. On the inside, I was anxiously waiting for my mom to leave, so I could finally unzip the stud. As soon as she dropped me off and departed, the full manifestation of the stud broke out. I was home alone in my apartment, due to my roommate living in town, and school wasn't set to begin for a few more days. This was perfect because I had time to get adjusted to my own identity without any interference. I resided in Windchester apartments; we had a basketball court, tennis court, and a swimming pool. Between me and my roommate, our two-bedroom, one bathroom apartment was fully furnished. I roamed from room to room, wondering what to do with myself. I hadn't met anyone on the team yet, so I just stayed inside and got to know the person who had been locked up. I was excited to call a few of my friends, and tell them that I was finally free, and that it was on and popping.

I immediately found my hat that had been hidden in my

suitcase, grabbed my bandana, and cocked my hat to the left. I was going to pretend to be a four-corner hustler by making them think I was in a gang. I didn't have a lot of baggy jeans, so I was in need of a store quick because I needed to do a wardrobe change. I didn't want anything girly, so I quickly began getting rid of anything that was too girly. My hair was growing, and I was able to braid it, or put it into two French braids. I put on some basketball shorts, Jordan's, a t-shirt, and my hat. I stood in the mirror posing for pics and was excited that I finally looked like a real dude. I looked like the studs I had seen throughout high school. I was holding my ball and somehow I felt like I had the look-down pack. I was studded out, and I had pride in my appearance. I didn't fear anyone's opinion because I had already survived all those stages in high school. I was finally able to be free.

I walked on my balcony, and from a distance, I spotted two black girls walking into an apartment, carrying luggage. I wondered if they were on the team, but I just chilled and figured I would find out later. I saw a lot of different people unloading and moving into their apartment. I figured I would stay inside my apartment until Monday, and would meet everybody when school began. I was anxious to meet a few people and see what college life was all about. I went over to the basketball court and shot some hoops, then went back to the apartment. I felt so grown, so adult like. It was weird- no curfew, no one watching over me, no one telling me what to do. I was really grown, and I didn't have to ask permission, I could literally do whatever I wanted. Wow, culture shock alright. I was hyped up, and ready to do me. Sunday evening my roommate arrived to move in because we had school the next day. When she walked in the door with her parents, she hesitated and looked shocked. I said, "Hey sup." You could tell they struggled. Not only was she moving in with a black girl, but a gay one at that. I picked up a weird vibe, but in my mind I was like, hey, deal with it or not, it's your choice because I'm going to do me. Diana moved in and was very quiet, she didn't say much, and neither did I. Turns out she was not only my roommate, but she was also the starting point guard, and I was vying for her position.

"I loved every moment of being different, and capturing the attention of so many. Whenever I walked into the class-room, into the cafeteria, or stepped foot into the gym, all eyes were on Sophia."

Monday morning, the first day of college, wow I'm on my own. I could wake up, get dressed, and put on whatever I wanted without fear of my mother's opinion. What an amazing feeling—freedom, freedom, freedom. Finally, I can be myself. I can break out of this shell and bring out the hidden being that's been hiding in isolation for years. Baggy shorts, boxers, tube socks, wife beater (tank-top), two corn-rows, red bandana, and red baseball hat. I stared myself in the mirror, smiled, rubbed my hands together, grabbed my ball, and pimped out the door, making sure I walked with a level of coolness. I was feeling good about myself. I felt like one of the boys, and I dared anyone to say anything to me. I smiled, laughed, and wandered the campus boldly.

Many of the students and teachers were shocked when they did attendance, called my name, and I responded. When I responded, "Here," other students would turn their heads and look at me shockingly. Some would whisper, "Wow, that's a girl." The teachers would even ask if I was sure. I wasn't embarrassed, nor ashamed, I was actually feeling good that they couldn't identify me as male or female. That was evidence that I was on the right track towards becoming the stud I longed to be.

There weren't many African-American's at the school, so whenever I saw an African-American I was excited to connect with my people. People clung to me, and I was cool with everybody, because I was loud, fun and out of control. I guess I was something different, because there weren't many homosexuals in the community, especially none that were out of the closet and bold as I was. I loved every moment of being different, and capturing the attention of so many. Whenever I walked into the classroom, into the cafeteria, or stepped foot into the gym, all eyes were on Sophia.

Many whispers, smirks, eye rolling, and gestures stirred me up to give them something to talk about. My name was in everybody's mouth, folks wanted to know where I was from, who I was, and how I was so boldly walking around claiming to be gay. Claiming to be gay, no claiming, this is exactly who I am. The women were full of curiosity, and

I just waited for the opportune time. I decided to spend my freshman year adjusting to college life, and familiarizing myself with my environment. I met a lot of guys from Mt. Vernon and started kicking it with a diverse group of people.

There were two other African-American females on the basketball team. They were roommates, and came from the same area, so they knew one another very well. I hung out with them, and we had a strong friendship. Freshman year at Open Lake was nothing like high school. No one was really talking about homosexuality except for me. It was like I was openly pioneering perversion in the region. Whenever we went to stores, restaurants, or anywhere, people would literally stare at me in disbelief that I was so bold about my sexuality. I didn't care what anyone thought. In my opinion, these people didn't know me, and I didn't care what they thought. If I wanted to make advances on a woman, it would always be a female who didn't play ball. I took a halt on dating and just dived into school and basketball. I also worked in the fitness center, so I was exposed to meeting different women who came to work out.

Most of the ladies would spend time chatting with me since I worked in the gym and played basketball. I seized every moment to plant a seed by making gestures, and saying something sexual about their bodies. Some of the women would smile, and say you're so cute while some just simply ignored my comments. I found it funny how some of the ladies who boldly proclaimed they were straight, and only liked men, they faithfully hungered for my words of affirmation and validation. I began to understand the power of words, and learned skillfully how to make one pregnant with those words, with the intent to water that word on the next visit and within a few months I would have conquered her very soul. It became a game, a challenge, and I could feel the reinforcement of demonic favor supporting and endorsing me. After a while, I got bored with turning women out, it was a norm, and nothing new. I was in full-blown stud mode, and I was on a mission.

I Want to Go Home

Basketball conditioning had officially begun. High school hadn't prepared me for this at all. Conditioning in college was on a whole different level. No longer was I the star, who was guaranteed the starting point guard position, I had to earn my spot. The practices were at six a.m., and the school was 15 minutes from my apartment, so every morning I had to be up by five a.m. What kind of stuff is this, I thought to myself. Transporting my school clothes to school, to dress after conditioning, then off to my eight o'clock class. This is crazy, is all I thought, but I had to get the starting position. Therefore, I had to put in work.

We would arrive at school, and the coaches would be outside in their cars waiting for us to put our stuff away, stretch and head back outside. Outside, what are we going to do outside? It's way too cold to be outside. Why aren't we running inside the gym? I don't mind doing a few killers, but why outside. A look of confusion would set in on my face, but I had to stand strong, and act like it was no big deal, when in reality it was a huge deal.

The coach had a stopwatch in his hand and a whistle. One car in front of us, and one behind us. We were given directions to run 2.5 miles, around the cornfields in a certain amount of time, and if we didn't make the time we had to do it again. I assumed it wouldn't be a problem until I turned the first curve, cold wind hitting my chest, sweat dripping off my forehead and my heart burning. I got to stop, I can't do this anymore, I'm done. I hated running and not being able to see the finish line. The team was screaming, " Run Sophia, let's go, you can do it." The more they called my name, the angrier I became. Conditioning was hard for me, and I felt like I was going to die out there. After conditioning, we would go inside the gym, and begin preparing for practice. Basketball on the collegiate level was something new. It wasn't anything I was prepared for, and I began to struggle. I wasn't used to being the underdog. I had been spoiled in high school and had everything served to me. Now I had to earn a name for myself, and the coach appeared to be disconnected from me. He wasn't the man excited to get me to his school, he had changed, now he was cheering on everyone else but me, so I thought. All of a sudden, the desire to leave, started playing over and over in my head. Then this happened.

Things began to take a turn for the worse. Being a freshman in college, away from my family, and on my own was beginning to take a toll on me. I mean, don't get me wrong, it felt great being on my own and being free. However, I was tired of dealing with the coach. I felt like the he was way too hard on me, and I wanted to go home.

Mom Come Get Me

I got into a verbal altercation with my roommate/team-mate, and I felt like the coach was taking her side. She was a sophomore and was the starting point guard. We went hard against one another practice after practice, and in my opinion, I was better than she was. She had a strong relationship with the coach, was the captain of the team, and Coach was allowing her to get away with murder. After practice, I made up in my mind that I was going home. Forget this small, prejudice school, is what I said to myself. I'm going back to the city, forget these people. So I showed my tail at the end of practice. I disrespected both the team and the coach. My rage and anger escalated to the point that I wanted to fight. I ran out and called my mother, crying, hyperventilating, and commanding my mother to come pick me up. I screamed I'm ready to come home now as I explained everything that was going on. With a voice of certainty, my mother respond-ed, "I'll be there tomorrow; momma is on her way." I felt so good because I experienced a sense of relief as if a weight had fallen off my shoulders. My mother assured me that she would be there to pick me up, so I did exactly what I'd wanted to do for three weeks, and that's curse everybody out. I started saying, "Forget it all, I'm going home, my mother coming to pick me up." I kicked the locker, stormed out of the gym, and headed back to my apartment. Before my teammate could drop me off at my apartment, I had jumped out the car, and ran up a flight of stairs, keys dropping out my hand, and heart pounding with anticipation of leaving. I began gathering all of my items, and packing my clothes, well not packing, I was stuffing and jamming stuff into bags. I had all my stuff stacked up against the wall- my television, microwave, toaster, and more, all set and ready to roll.

"When I looked in the mirror, I didn't recognize the Sophia that had been in high school, I was developing into a stud, and the attention drew me further and further into the life."

After multiple hours, it was becoming darker and darker outside, and my mom still hadn't arrived. Where is she I wondered, I thought she was coming. What's going on? So I paced back and forth around my apartment, waiting for my mother to pull up with her friend, to pick her baby up. What could possibly be taking her so long, I mean don't she know I'm in a crisis. The later it became, the more my stomach ached and cramped. Disappointment began to set in, and I thought to myself this can't be happening, surely my mother is coming.

Every time I heard a car pull up, saw lights or heard a door slam, I said oh there she goes. Nope, still not her. Finally, I called home, and my mom answered the phone. My heart dropped, and I was so confused. "Mom where are you, why are you still at home, what are you doing. Come get me, I hate it here," I screamed and cried, "Hurry mom, my stuff is packed, please come and pick me up." My mother responded, "You can do it, just stick it out." She then stated, "Mrs. Love warned me you would call, and told me not to pick you up." I was furious and hurt; I couldn't believe my mom was refusing to pick me up. I just had to do something about this. I was backed into a corner, there was no way I could return to the team, I had cursed everyone out, so that option was over.

Five minutes into me thinking of a Plan B to get home, I heard a knock on the door. I hesitated, then I slowly approached the door, peeked out the peephole, and Coach Wells was at the door. I opened the door, and with a huge smile, he said, "Okay kiddo, you ready to apologize and move forward because your mom isn't coming to pick you up." My feet felt like they were sinking in quicksand. Pride gripped my heart, and there was no way I was going to apologize. Coach reminded me of my future, my destiny, and why I was at Open Lake, and something in me stirred up. I agreed to show up at practice the next day to apologize to everyone, and ask to be back on the team. I truly learned a valuable lesson regarding humility. The team greeted me with open arms, and that was a turning point in my life. The "I wanna go home" tantrum, slowly but surely vanished. I was now ready to work hard, and become the athlete I knew I was created to become.

ADJUSTING TO COLLEGE LIFE

After a few months of becoming adjusted, and preparing for basketball season, I spent time getting used to the freedom I had. I was attending college parties, drinking, smoking and engaging in sexual acts. I was attending parties with the fellas, and when the drinking began, sex was attached. It was as if the women were attracted to me like a magnet, based on me looking like one of the fellas, but having the compassion of a woman. They would laugh, get drunk, and snicker with one another about who was going to sleep with me. I began to evolve more and more into the homosexual lifestyle; however, because I was so free to be me, I wasn't focused so much on women like I was in high school. I was now focused on basketball, and developing into a solid point guard, to ensure I received a scholarship for the next level. During my freshman and sophomore years in college, I began dating women, having sex, and converting others to the homosexual lifestyle. College life for me was about independence, basketball, and sex. I enjoyed my freedom, and of course, basketball was my focus, but women became my main attraction.

I began to realize after having sex with whomever I wanted, that it was no longer about the sex. I was different, I didn't desire to be with anyone on the basketball team, and I wasn't attracted to gay girls, my eyes were set on the challenge of conversion. I was becoming well known on the team, at school and even in the community. I was becoming more and more masculine and dominate. When I looked in the mirror, I didn't recognize the Sophia that had been in high school, I was developing into a stud, and the attention drew me further and further into the life.

Humbled Real Quick

I spent endless hours in practice, so it was difficult trying to juggle a personal life and basketball. I focused on the season and kept my gaze fixed on balling. The first game of the season when the coach revealed the starting lineup, I was devastated that I wasn't a starter. Heck, I thought, I was one of the best players on the team, how in the world am I not starting. I was angry, and again I wanted to quit the team and go home. Instead of crying about it, I pushed and was determined to crack into the starting lineup by the second half of the season. Parents would make negative comments in the stands about me, by pointing and calling me gay. My team didn't have any studs my freshman year, however, when we played other schools, I witnessed a stud on almost every team. I worked hard developing a relationship with Coach, paying attention to his orders, and determining in my heart that I would be a starter soon. Once I adjusted my attitude, things began to work in my favor. My coach believed in me more; I was getting increased playing time, and before the second half, I was pushing point guard. Yesssss, now I'm one more step closer to my dream. Basketball season was going well, and I was getting more adjusted to college life.

One of the most difficult parts about college was deciding

home, I had my earphones in and was rocking to some Jay-Z, Twista, and Tupac. Head nodding and feeling good, keeping my mind free from distracting thoughts regarding what my family would say when I made it home. The music drowned out all of my thoughts and stimulated my adrenaline that I would be okay just doing me.

When I got off the train, panic gripped my heart; sweat rolled down my forehead, and once again my nose was sweating like a water fountain had been poured over it. I quickly took my hat off, stuffed it into my pocket, pulled my pants up to tighten my belt, and ran into the bathroom, and attempted to take a wet brush to brush my pretties down. I tried to girly myself a tad bit, but it wasn't working. I slowly walked outside to get in the car with my mother and godmother. They were happy to see me, but I could feel in my stomach, that my mother wasn't comfortable with how I looked. She didn't say one word about my sexuality, but I could feel the weight of her embarrassment. I decided to press past what I was feeling, and focus on spending time with my family. I took over the conversation by talking about basketball, college life, and going on and on about how the season was going.

Once we made it to my mother's home, I pulled my luggage inside. I ran straight to my room, because I didn't want to make myself so visible. It was like I was hiding all over again. My mother didn't mention anything about my sexual preference, however, almost every day she would make a comment about what I had on. She couldn't stand how I was dressed, and I knew she didn't want me going around her family looking like this. I was thinking of an excuse to get out of the house, so I connected with some of my old teammates. When we got together, it was all good. Sophia was in full stud mode when we hit the streets. I got back on the party line and hooked up with a few ladies while I was home. I decided to spend my time at my sister's home because she allowed me to be myself. She didn't question my sexuality, and she certainly never made me feel insecure about my style of dress. It was difficult being so free, only to return home and be so bound.

Coming home for the holidays became stressful, to where I got to the point of not wanting to come home on breaks. I hated turning my personality on and off, being free and bold in college, then coming home and trying to downplay my sexuality. My mother loved me, and she never said anything in reference to my sexuality, but as a daughter, I knew my mom wasn't pleased with how I looked. Each break, things got better and better for me. I stopped hiding my identity and boldly allowed myself to be free at home. My mother loved me and supported my basketball career. She wanted me to be delivered, but she didn't shove it down my throat. My mother was more embarrassed about my lifestyle because of her fears of what the family would think. I decided instead of putting so much shame on the family; it was in my best interest not to come home on all holiday breaks.

Immediately after leaving home, and returning to school, it felt good to be free. Back to normal, no worries, thoughts or wonders on how my mother would feel. The only person's opinion I was concerned about was my mother's. My father and mother were separated, so I didn't see my father on a daily basis, but when I did he didn't say anything about my sexuality or my image. He was just cool with everything. I don't even think I ever shared with my dad that I was gay. I just allowed him to assume, so we never touched the subject. My extended family had opinions, and didn't like the way I dressed and made comments, but I didn't care, I was only concerned about what my mother thought about me.

Note to Parents:

The reason your child is not coming around as they used to is not that they don't love you, but it's easier to be themselves in your absence. Most children have respect for their parents, and it's easier to keep a distance and be free than to be bound by parent's opinions. Your child does not come around because of the restraints put on them by your opinions.

Second Semester

The second half of the season went well. I was more adjusted to college life and was comfortable. I established a relationship with the coach, and he was even taking my advice about bringing two girls from Chicago to join us next year. I was hoping this would happen because I was bored being the only stud on the team. It wasn't as fun as I thought it would be. I mean I had a great time being myself, and didn't have any problems getting into a relationship, however, I wanted a running buddy, someone like me to join the squad. The two girls I was considering weren't out the closet regarding their sexual preference. However, I knew before long they would be free as a bird, and would come out about their identities. Basketball season went well. I was starting consistently at the second half of the season and was looking into my future after Open Lake. I spent the second half of the season working out, building muscle, and developing my skills.

My dream of being a professional basketball player was becoming more real. Our team wasn't the greatest. However, I used my freshman year to adjust to the collegiate level, gain experience and prepare for the next level. I continued to work in the gym and spent long hours there perfecting my handles and my jumper. Splash, splash, splash nothing but net. I was beginning to taste success and often got high off the fantasy of playing professionally. At this point, I was fully engaged in a relationship. I wasn't trying to figure out my identity, and I had become the very thing I dreamed of becoming, the best stud I could be. I no longer needed any teaching on how to develop into a stud. I was a stud. I was living my life to the fullest, and life was going well. I was comfortable in my skin at this point.

My life began to slow down, as I would go to class, practice, then return home. I got into a routine of chilling and slowing my pace down. I didn't have to strive to look for women, and I wasn't running around trying to figure out my identity. I spent time watching movies and games and

I didn't know anything about a personal relationship with God. Other than saying the sinner's prayer as a child and being baptized, I was sort of out of the loop with God. Now my mind was wondering about God, and whether or not I was going to hell. I couldn't silence the voice in my head, and in my heart, something had been turned on, and I couldn't shut it off. I remember thinking to myself; I'm too young to worry about this God stuff and eternity. I didn't think about death. I felt that I would get my life together when I got older, and then I would be good about going to heaven. As of now, I wanted to live my life, play basketball, go to the WNBA, and maybe one day marry a woman. I didn't have any intentions on getting caught up with the God chatter. The louder the convictions, the louder the enemy, screamed and seduced my heart to keep living in my sin.

"Basketball was the gateway to homosexuality, the bridge for anyone to cross over into it. I was a magnet, and many of the girls came and sat at my table to eat the words I was feeding them."

The enemy continued to torment me and tell me that hell wasn't real and that if God didn't want me gay, he wouldn't have made me this way. I was swallowing the words of the enemy, and although his words were bitter, they were sweet as honey to my mouth, and I believed every word he declared over my life. I was promised that if I stayed in the homosexual lifestyle, I would go to the WNBA. I would be the face of the league, and I could have any woman I wanted. I was promised money, success, and fame. I began to honor his words because his language was confirmation to my hearts desires.

Sophomore year I felt like I was in a tug of war with my destiny and my purpose. I was on a mission as I blocked out the opinions of others. I was determined to take my basketball career to the next level. I was the starting point guard, and at this point, my reputation was well known in the community. I was the talk of the city. I was invited into the bedchambers and upper rooms to sleep with women. Curiosity was at an all-time high, and I was being approached by women of every breed. It was as if the enemy had launched a missile to stroke my ego, and to be honest, it worked. Slowly the convictions I once had became silent, and my appetite and craving for wickedness increased. I was playing basketball with a passion, my skills on and the off the court were drastically improving, and I was moving towards increasing my stud profile, especially before going to a university. Most of the studs I witnessed playing on other teams had tattoos and piercings, so I decided it was time to tat up my body and get a few piercings. I got my tongue pierced and two tattoos.

I felt superior and like I had a sense of control, power, authority, and justification. Like a vampire, I was dark, and I longed to suck the blood and life out of anyone willing to lay with me. I knew the power and influence I had and my capabilities to convert. It was never about the sex and never about the affection, something in me shifted, and everything was about the conversion. The enemy made me feel supernatural.

I was able to shift and alter one's way of living to be with me.

After I had come into agreement with this new awakening, I felt empowered on the court and was ready to take on my opponent to see what was in store for my future. I was moving in a new power, with a new thrust. I felt some sort of endorsement. The enemy showed me the WNBA. I saw the spirit of homosexuality and how it connected with basketball, and I wanted in on this move. I wanted in on this.

When the season began, I was playing with a different attitude. I felt help from a strange place, but this feeling was overtaking me. I was operating from a place of power. My influence was rising on and off the court. I was dropping points on the court, and dropping seeds of perversion in the imaginations of any woman who came into my presence. When women would come towards me asking questions, I gave them descriptive responses with the intent to impregnate their imagination with my words. Even if they weren't sexually active with me, I knew if I spoke words into their imagination, they would play with those words, and those words would manifest by them seeking those words again. I sat in the locker room and although I had no intention to sleep with my teammates, the locker room was full of demonic words of perversion.

Basketball was the gateway to homosexuality, the bridge for anyone to cross over into it. I was a magnet, and many of the girls came and sat at my table to eat the words I was feeding them. I desired to make one full off of my words, so when they departed, they would hunger for more. I moved in this realm throughout my sophomore year, and I began to impact the city. I was able to shift a region with my presence, and when I left the region, my footprints were set, and I was well known in the land.

I finished the season as the starting point guard. A university recruited me. I knew the moment I met the recruiter that I was interested in doing a visit, based on the coach who came to scout me. Finally, a female coach who was in the life. I was eager to shift from Open Lake College to the next level. I graduated from junior college with an Associate's Degree in Criminal Justice. I desired to work with children who were in the juvenile justice system and felt that I could connect to them acting out because they were unable to articulate the trauma they were enduring.

I was now another step closer to achieving my goal to be in the WNBA. Let's get it.

CHAPTER 6
UNIVERSITY

I was one step closer to my dream. I'd overcome much adversity, and all I had was two more years to do before going to the pros. I was the starting point guard, and captain my junior and senior year. I lived in a gated, four-bedroom apartment. Located on Natural Bride Road, the university was huge. I was excited because Nelly from the St. Lunatics was popular, along with Chingy, so I felt some type of connection to the city. After arriving at the university, I was exposed to homosexuality on another level in the basketball arena. Both of my coaches were gay, and the head coach was in a relationship. Her girlfriend would come to games, and we were all cool with her. It was awesome being on a team, and around other homosexuals. From the cheerleaders to the band members, these girls were all over me. I wasn't pursuing a relationship, so I just dropped seeds of perversion, that tormented their minds, and all they would do is desire me to be with them. I was flattered by my ability to convert, and have one toss and turn with desire for something I wasn't willing to give them.

College life was fun. There were so many different people there, a diverse crowd, people from every nation and tribe. I was popular because I played basketball and hung out with so many people. The squad was full of studs, and our locker room and bus chats were full of perversion, with me being one of the ringleaders. The coaches didn't care what we talked about. One of the coaches was cool with us talking, and she would often chime in on what we were discussing. The bus rides were long trips from state to state, place to place, and some of the girls would be sexing right on the bus. It was nothing to witness perversion take place on the bus. It was normal. The boys team rode the bus with us as well, and there were times when some of the girls who were straight would mess around on the bus. Sex was the center of attention, and the bus rides were hot and heavy with perversion. The dudes were cool about us being gay; they didn't make comments or say anything. I actually talked their language, and it was all good.

The higher you rose in basketball the more perversion you would see. Basketball was serious. The coaches took the game seriously, and conditioning, training, and weight lifting were no joke. We put in work. Early workouts, late workouts, weekend practices, I mean we did all. I was pushed to the max, and the harder I worked, the cockier I became. Basketball was strengthening my masculinity, and my level of sexual identity was being confirmed. Straight or not you were exposed to homosexuality at a high level in the basketball world. It's amongst you, it's in your face, and you are the minority if you're not involved in it. There was always someone after the straight ones. They were targets, and escaping being approached, and pressured was slim to none. All gay girls were not studs, the feminine ones were able to mask it, but the studs got the most attention because of their outer appearance. No matter where you go to play in the basketball arena, you would see homosexuality- whether it's the players on the team, coach on the sideline, or girlfriends in the crowd. It was normal, popular, and a part of the game.

Playing basketball opens the door in so many ways to being a homosexual. You are surrounded by a group of women who think like you think, and feel like you feel.

While at the university, I was exposed to drag queens, transgenders, and the club scene. I was in a club every Saturday night. We would go to one club at midnight, leave at 3 AM, then head to another from 3 a.m. to 6 a.m. I was clubbing, having a ball, and was drunk off the adrenaline of so many homosexuals all under one roof. It was nothing to be in the club and witness people having sex right in the middle of club. It was an entirely new level, and it pushed me further into the life.

My junior year I decided it was time to take my look to another level. I cut my hair into a fade, sliced my eyebrows, put designs in my head, and upped my swag. I was wearing name brand everything from head to toe. Rocking Timberland boots and sweaters, I was attracting a whole new crowd. I remember going to apply for financial aid, and one of the advisors who was married glared at me and asked if she could take care of me. She told me how she'd seen me around campus, and wanted to know if I could help her get in shape by helping her with weights. She was an older woman, sophisticated, and very well educated. To be honest, I was flattered, and desired to assist her, but I wasn't sure where this was going. So I began training with her two days a week for a few weeks. During this time, she would tell me about her marriage and discuss her problems. I would listen and be a voice. I didn't want to cross boundaries, so I just listened.

After a few weeks, I decided to respond and began sharing with her that she needed a woman, someone who understood her, and who would take care of her needs emotionally over sexually. She was engaged and eating my very words. After a few more conversations, she stopped showing up at the gym to train with me. I wondered what happened, what I said, what did I do. I caught up with her and asked if I had done something wrong, and she responded, "No, you said everything right, so I can't work out any further because I don't want to cross boundaries." She expressed how much she thought of me, and it was dangerous to continue talking. Right then I realized how powerful my ability was to change lives. I didn't want anything to do with this woman. However, I was flattered, and this gave me momentum.

Perversion was at an all-time high. We would be clubbing, and would run into one of the coaches at the club. One of my teammates danced with one of the coaches, and boundaries were crossed. I thought it was cool, that my teammate was able to pull one of the coaches. I'm not sure what happened with that relationship, but things were getting out of control at the club. Life was great—basketball, clubs, and women. I was living my dream. I was in love with my life and had no plans on giving up this dream. I wasn't thinking about no God, and I wasn't caught up in anyone's opinion. Even when I began going home, it was no longer a problem. I was open with who I was. I would go home just the way I was. I didn't work extra hard to clean myself up. However, it was something about when I went home for breaks; I wasn't so dark. It was as if God gave me grace when I was around my mother. I was caught up in my world. I was the starting point guard, and one step away from my dream becoming a reality. I wasn't going to be sidetracked or distracted at all; I was just trying to get to the league.

Playing basketball opens the door in so many ways to being a homosexual. You are surrounded by a group of women who think like you think, and feel like you feel. Especially when dealing with studs, because behind every stud is a story. A story of pain, rejection, abandonment and trauma. While basketball is a game, it's also a gateway to open you up to the spirit of homosexuality on another level. You feel validated because others are dealing with similar stories as you, and it reinforces what you feel. When coaches and people of influence who have gone before you confirm what you're feeling is normal, it impacts and assures you that you're okay. The idea that you're going through a phase, shifts and you begin to swallow and digest the words that this is the way you were born. Behind the heart of every hardcore stud is a little girl desperately crying out for help, attention, protection, validation and affirmation. Basketball becomes her strong tower, her mask, and her place of safety during a time of trouble. She's scarred with wounds of rejection, and bleeding with pain, so she covers her scars by putting on an identity of protection. When she gets around other women who have gone before her or have been through what she's been through it confirms her lifestyle and image. Basketball is a release, yet it gives one a sense of control. Basketball for me was my security, my release, and my strong tower. Running point guard taught me a lot. I was responsible for leading a team, controlling the tempo and so much more, you will learn more about this later in the book.

My experience at the University secured and wrapped me into homosexuality on a new level. There are dimensions to perversion, and I felt like I was growing and expanding to new levels. I was moving up in rank, and the higher you go athletically, the higher rank you have in the demonic realm. The spirit of homosexuality has realms to it, just like the spirit realm. I was entering new realms as my influence increased. I was excited about completing my college years, and moving forward to the league. I knew I would have some adversity, due to me not going to a major university, so I was prepared to try out for the league no matter what steps I had to take. Everything was perfect until this happened:

One day I was at home for a holiday break, and I was hanging out with my godmother. We stopped at her sister's home for a quick visit, and while I was there, I was attempting to call one of my friends, but she wasn't answering the phone. I went to sit down on the couch to wait on my godmother when this young girl, who was deaf and unable to speak, appeared out of nowhere. She immediately stood in front of me and was moving her hands swiftly, pointing her finger, and pointing up to the ceiling. I'm looking like, what's up with this little girl. I was scared because I had never witnessed such a thing. I quietly leaned back on the couch. I had on a red jacket, Timberland boots, Enyce jeans, and my hair had 360 waves.

My heart began to pound; my stomach started hurting, and of course my nose began sweating. I had a gut feeling that something wasn't right. However I played it off and asked if someone could tell me what was going on. The little girl's mother looked at me and said, "Oh you don't want to know." I became curious and begged someone to interpret that moment. So the mother took me into the room with the little girl and my godmother's sister. During this time, the little girl began doing it again with an angry passion. I couldn't understand what her problem was. Then the mother stated, "The Lord says why do you hurt Him? Why won't I come to him? Why am I living in a condition that he has already set me free from?" I said to myself, this is a freaking set up, surely the Lord isn't asking me questions when he already knows the answer. I was furious at this point. Then suddenly the little girl started saying that the Lord loves me and that he created me to be a woman, in his image. I still wasn't buying it.

Finally, the little girl was able to tell me exactly who I was calling, and why the person wasn't answering the phone. She hit me with a prophetic word of knowledge. At this point, water filled my eyes, and if I blinked, I would have flooded the floors. I rushed out and begged my god mom to get me out of there. We departed, and my entire world was turned upside down. I was confused, sad, scared and didn't know how to respond. I was freaked out because I had never seen such a thing before. I didn't know what to think, how could I share this moment with anyone, they would think I was crazy. "Heck, am I crazy, what's wrong with me," I thought. I couldn't wait to get back to school, because now here came those feelings of conviction, and the desire to speak to this God with whom I had no relationship. Uggggggh, she had just messed me up. I was in need of a blunt to suppress these new feelings. How could this happen when life for me was going great. I was living my best life, so I thought.

When I returned to school, something different was happening. I was carrying around this feeling of what is God thinking. What am I going to do, I couldn't tell my homies this stuff. I was looking in the mirror trying to wash off the confusion; I was like a deer in headlights. This little girl came along and knocked me unconscious from my life, and shifted me into a new place. I was on an emotional roller coaster, and once again these God thoughts became a distraction. People were asking, "Sophia what's wrong with you?" I had to play it cool, and say, " Oh nothing. I'm good." I figured I'd be back to normal once I went to the club. About a week later I went to the club with one of my homies. I got dressed, as usual, listening to some N-SYNC and jamming. I was creating my atmosphere before I made it to the club.

As soon as we arrived, I felt some type of way. I felt bad about going to the club, and in my head, I began repenting and apologizing to God. Oh no, what am I doing? Why am I concerned with God? I battled in my mind over and over, trying to make myself comfortable. I was beginning to get uncomfortable in my own skin. I was drinking and smoking weed to take my focus away from my discomfort. Once I began smoking and drinking it increased because it kept my mind off of my convictions. That encounter pulled me out of a realm, and now I was developing a sensitivity, and I was more aware of my feelings. It was as if those words had pulled off a bandage, and I was able to feel the blood. I strived to get back to that dark place, but the words of God saying that he loved me, chased me down like a hurricane. I wondered if God really loved me, and I began asking myself why did he love, and how could he love me. After a few weeks of this, I was able to drown out the sound of God, because the volume of the enemy increased. He reminded me that the little girl was deaf and convinced me that the little girl's mother was speaking on her behalf, and was making up stuff. Suddenly I shook off that experience, and came into agreement that it wasn't God.

Wow, I can breathe again. Back to normal and back to my old self again. Just to think, I almost gave into that experience. I was back hitting the clubs and doing Sophia. Basketball season came to an end, and I was set to graduate college with my bachelor's degree in criminal justice. It had been an unbelievable experience, and I was the first person on my father's side to graduate from college. I didn't want to go back to Chicago, and I wasn't going straight to the WNBA, so I was forced to decide on a plan b. I met a man in Mt. Vernon, who agreed to be my personal trainer, and assist me with a WNBA tryout. I got a job at an emergency shelter for children while I trained and awaited what my future entailed. I was determined and knew that this was just another hurdle before launching to the WNBA. I considered going overseas.

However, 9/11 had recently occurred, and I was afraid to go to a foreign country, so I just declared that I would strive to make the league. I graduated from college and was on the road to pursue my destiny. I knew that all the adversity to make it to the WNBA would pay off. Surely I wasn't enduring such adversity for no reason. I continued to remind myself that the strongest survived. I was determined to stretch and advance to the next level. I was willing to sacrifice it all to pursue my dream. I never returned home to Chicago after college. My mother assumed I would return home, get a job, and pursue my dream from there, but I was too free to go back to the bondage of living under the rules or her opinion of my lifestyle. Although my mother didn't give me a hard time, I didn't want to expose her to my darkness.

College life at the university was much different from my junior college experience. On the junior college level, other than having independence, it was still like high school. Yet in both places, the spirit of homosexuality escalated, the higher I went athletically. The exposure was heightened and the doors were open to engaging in wickedness on a new level. I was going to miss college life, but I was determined to pursue my passion, unhindered and undistracted. I developed so much wisdom on being a point guard. It was more than just basketball, having point guard skills had become my way of life. College life was a dream come true. I did everything I dreamed about as a kid. Although I had obstacles, I still persevered and accomplished my dream. I graduated from college, I broke the curse off my bloodline, I played the game I loved on the college level, and I unleashed my inner stud. In my opinion, life was great, and I was on the road to it getting even better.

Chapter 7
Let the Training Begin

*N*ow that college was over, I didn't have the discipline of a coach screaming in my ear to get to practice. I didn't have anyone forcing me to run, condition, work on my handles, or push myself to the limit. I no longer had the support of a team telling me I could do it, push, work out, go hard. Everything from this point on was on me. I had to use my passion, my love, and my desire to be great to push me to the next level. I didn't have anyone setting the pace or tempo of my conditioning. No one cared at this point if I continued or if I decided to drop the ball and quit. This time of my life was a testing of my heart. Did I really want it and how bad did I want it? I had to awaken discipline and pull out every word of correction, encouragement, and wisdom I had learned from my coaches over the years. I had to put in the work even when no one was looking. I couldn't cheat the suicide sprints. I couldn't lie about running a mile without walking. I couldn't lie about shooting 100 free throws. If I lied, I would only be cheating myself, and I would be affecting my own personal progress, and not the teams. It was all about Sophia at this time of my life. This moment had no effect on anyone other than me. I was in it to win it; I was determined. I wanted to make the WNBA with every fiber in my body. Every morning my feet hit the floor, I could feel my moment of success getting closer and closer. I wanted to make the league so bad; I decided to get a tattoo on my leg that represented my desperation, as a daily reminder to pursue my dream with everything in me. I got praying hands with a ball over it, and a light going around the ball, with the word "sacrifice" inscribed beneath the praying hands. I was determined to pray until I made it. I was determined to risk my life, and to sacrifice, and abandon everything to make this team. Whatever I had to give up, I was willing. I would recklessly abandon all for my chance to make the league.

I put in work. I began training by going to the track and running a mile, sprinting, and doing suicides with my friend Devon and Racine. I ran until my sweat dripped blood. I ran with intensity and worked out, lifting weights until my muscles felt like jelly. I was up early running, and going to bed late running. I studied plays, and I would spend hours watching videos of other girls playing in the league. I worked on my handles day in and day out. I worked on my vision by dribbling blindfolded. I played daily, and not a day went by that I wasn't on the court. I ran until I puked, and even if my chest burned I pushed myself to the limit. I pushed passed how I felt, kept my eyes fixed on the prize, and I knew that the moment would come when my name would be called be placed on a WNBA team. I didn't care if others thought it was impossible for me to achieve my goal, I was determined to keep pushing. I learned perseverance, endurance, and stamina. I wasn't moved by distractions; I kept moving forward. I pushed against the weights that appeared unmovable. I was positioned for success. I challenged myself daily and got better each day.

I got a personal trainer to assist me with taking my skills to another level. This man went to work at 5 a.m., so the only time he had available to train me was from 3-4 a.m. We were granted access to a school gym for workouts, and I met him every morning at 3. This man pushed me beyond my comprehension. I was angry with him because he pushed me out of my comfort zone, and stretched muscles in me that I didn't realize were there. He challenged me to rise up and take my game to the next level. He worked me out. He taught me how to handle the ball, how to overcome the noise, and to keep pushing. Training with him took me to another level. I was faithful to my 3 a.m. workouts. I learned discipline by getting to bed early, so I could rise at 2 a.m., get dressed, and make it to the gym by 3. I wasn't tired, and I didn't hesitate. I rose promptly because basketball was my heart, and I was willing to pay the price for success. I sacrificed rest, gave up meals, and even let go of friendships. I didn't care what it was; I just wanted to create a clear path for my dream to come true.

Many people doubted me, but I believed it was possible, and I was sure it would happen. I was confident that my dream would come true. Why wouldn't it, I mean everything else in my life was going as planned. Life was great, and I was on track to accomplish my dream. How could I not make it after putting in all this training on my own. I dreamed of returning to the community and showing where I had worked out, and sharing with other little girls that it's possible to accomplish their dream, no matter what curve balls you're handed. I was a success story in the making. I continued intense training for a few months before the professional tryout in San Jose, California, for the semi-pro WNBA team. It was a once in a lifetime dream.

We got to the last month and a half before the tryout, when my trainer stopped coming to the gym. He didn't call me and he gave me no notice that he had quit. I was devastated, how could he just quit on me when I was so close to the finish line. Oh well, I couldn't quit, it wasn't his dream, it was mine. I was determined to keep pushing myself. I ran full court one on one by myself in the gym, pretending to be in a sold out arena with the game on the line. I lived for moments of pressure, and I longed for the challenges. I was going to be the comeback kid, the underdog who came completely out of nowhere and made the team. My name in lights, and the whole world wondering how I made it to the league. Those moments drove me to persevere. I could see the faces of little girls who felt it would be impossible until they heard the story of Sophia Ruffin. I could taste the moment. All eyes on Sophia. So I couldn't quit, I had come too far to turn back, and walk away from my dream. There was just no way.

All Eyes On Me

On my job at the shelter, I played ball with the kids and did mini-camps. The kids loved when I came to work because we spent endless hours at the rec. No misbehavior broke out on my shift because I was right there with the kids playing, and spending time with them. They were impressed because they knew I was going to make it to the WNBA. They were watching my life, and I was hope to the hopeless. I shared with them some of my life experiences, and they were like wow, if you can do it, so can I. I had all eyes on me. Even the staff believed I would make it. Back home, my family was counting on me. My nephew Marquese longed for his auntie to make the WNBA. He would always say, " Auntie when you make the team, buy me a computer." I had to make it. There were no other options for me. My life at this point was do or die, and I had to respond. I had no plan b for my life; this was it.

CHAPTER 8
ROAD TO DAMASCUS
(CONTACT WITH POWER)

$\mathscr{I}$ was headed to the barbershop in downtown Mt. Vernon to get my haircut. I was at the barbershop weekly. My barber cut my hair faithfully. He tapered it just right, and kept my lining on fleek. He was well-known in town for cutting hair, so I did my weekly trip to get cut up before hitting the club that night. I was on the phone with one of my homeboys who I was going to the club with, and we were making our plans for the night. I was surrounded by a shop full of men, but I didn't trip, everyone in town knew about me at this point. I was well-known in the region, so I wasn't ashamed or timid. I was shooting the breeze, laughing, and trying to get done, so I could go home and get dressed. It was nice outside, so I had on some Air Force 1's, some shorts, and a t-shirt. I was chilling, nothing major. As soon as I sat down in the chair, and he put the cape over me to begin cutting, I see this large, black man with big eyes, walk inside. I kept yapping and having a good time. All of a sudden someone says, "Hey Apostle," and all the men began speaking and hatting with him. I didn't know who this man was, so I didn't say too much. He sat down, and I don't know what happened to me. All of a sudden my neck got hot. My neck was sweating, my nose, and my forehead was dripping. I was having a panic attack, and couldn't figure out what was going on. I was choked up on my words, I mean I was getting upset because I couldn't make sense of what was happening to my body. It was as if this man had walked into the shop and my demons had come under his authority. I tried to manifest, but my demons were weakened. I just sat silent, and whispered to my barber to hurry up, so I could leave the shop. I couldn't wait to get out of that shop, or at least until that man left. "Who is this man?" I wondered, "Who is this with this much power and authority?" I couldn't figure it out. But whoever he was, he had jurisdiction because I was unable to respond the way I desired. As soon as my barber lined me up, I jumped out of my chair, paid him, and didn't wait for the change. I was thinking, "dude keep the change. I gotta get out of this place."

When I got inside my car, I was furious. I put on some Lil Wayne, blasted my music and pulled off. I was triggered because I couldn't understand why I was scared of this man. I was shaken up, but it was cool, I wasn't going to allow that to ruin my night, so I kept it moving. I shared with a few of my homies the incident, and people were telling me who he was and that he was an apostle. Heck, that didn't mean not one thing to me. I didn't even know what an apostle was. I only knew about pastors and reverends. I was clueless, so I just kept it moving. I thought it was funny, but I sure didn't want to see that joker again.

A few weeks later, I heard about this apostolic church. My friend Devon was beginning to go to church all the time, so while I was drinking, smoking and clubbing, she was taking her daughters to church. One day she said to me, "Sophia you really need to go to church." Church, I laughed at her, and shook it off like girl, please. You can go to church, but I'm not going to no church. And what church is this? I tried going to church a few times in Mt. Vernon, and none of them worked out for me.

> *"Sophia I think that is God calling you to the altar, go get prayer Sophia." I said, "No, no, no way. Surely this isn't God; this is something else."*

People were judging me because I was gay, and it was obvious based on my appearance, so they would preach gay messages, and totally mishandle me. I didn't want to be around a bunch of hypocrites who didn't have the love of God, and all they did was make judgments about gay people. No one took the time to minister to my broken soul; they used that moment as a platform to openly shame me by making gay jokes, and when I left, I felt worse than when I had walked in.

Many people offered to take me to church, and viewed me as their personal projects; I hated it. There was no purity whatsoever. I was the poster child, and if they could get me saved, that would boost their evangelistic ratings. So going to church was a no-go for me. I remember Devon returning from church, and telling me, "Oh my goodness Sophia, it's so good. This church is different, you will really like it." She went on to tell me that someone had prophesied to her, and I was wondering what in the world that was. The look on her face was glorious, and she was so excited about this God. I wanted that feeling, so I considered going the next week. On that Sunday morning the next week, Devon asked me if I wanted to go to church, and I screamed, "Girl, no." Later that morning, I called a friend and asked if she wanted to go with me. I was curious to see what was going on at this church, so I went.

When I arrived, I pulled up to this big place that was once an old movie theater, and I was getting myself situated to go inside. I had no clue what I was about to enter, but I was like whatever, surely it's not too bad. I mean it's not like I had never been to church before. I grew up in church, so I had nothing to fear. But there was something unusual was about this church, I felt afraid, just a little bit. I did a mirror check, put on my Carmex, brushed down my waves, and prepared to walk inside with my friend. Devon was already there, so I was going to surprise her by coming. I checked my swag before going inside. I dressed up with khaki pants, a button up tucked inside, Doc Martin shoes, and a fresh fade. My eyebrows were freshly sliced, and I was looking good.

I walked inside and immediately walked to the top of the balcony. I didn't even look around to see if any seats were up front, I hit the back without hesitation. I sat next to Devon and the girls. Devon was on my right, and my friend Samantha, who had come with me, was on my left. Church was going good, I guess. I observed everything and everyone before letting any guards down. I looked down and realized, "Oh crap, that's the man I seen in the barber shop." I was hesitant, and wondering what I had just gotten myself into.

As the service went on, and I could see different people standing in positions in multiple corners of the church, praying in a foreign language, and going hard. I'm looking around like what in the world is going on? I was getting nervous because I wasn't use to this. I looked over at Devon, and she was standing with her hands up. I sat wondering why she had her hands raised. I didn't get it at all. The service was coming to an end, and the apostle summoned everyone to stand all over the building. I didn't feel like standing, so I remained seated and watched everyone else go forth. People were staring at me with a look of, "Today is the day, we are going to get her today." I could just feel an atmosphere of someone wanting to capture my soul. I shut down and refused to engage. All I kept saying is when I get out of here, I'm not coming back.

The choir began singing, "Come and Lay Down the Burdens, You Have Carried," by Martha Munnizi. They were singing, people were speaking foreign languages, and folks were falling out at the altar. I said to myself, "Oh Lord, what is this?" I just knew I wasn't going down there. I listened to the apostle as he spoke into people's lives, and they fell out like flies. I was scared to death. The more they fell out, the more he flowed, and the more my heart panicked. I knew something was happening when my entire back became soaking wet from sweat. I wondered, what in the world is going on, please get me out of here. I was screaming on the inside, but I couldn't move. He then asked everyone to grab their neighbor's hands, so I held Devon and Samantha's hands, all while shaking like a leaf. My hands were so wet, surely it was leaving puddles in their hands. I clinched Devon's hand so tight, I was scared to death. I was still sitting down refusing to look up and refusing to get up. All of a sudden, I began to hyperventilate. I couldn't breathe, my chest was tight, I was breaking out in hot sweats, and I went into an anxiety attack. I looked up at Devon and said help me, I can't breathe Devon, please help me, I can't breathe. The more I asked for help, the more my breath was leaving my body. All I could hear in my ear is the song come lay your burdens down for he is here. I continued to plead for Devon's help. Devon turned and said, "Sophia I think that is God calling you to the altar, go get prayer Sophia." I said, "No, no, no way. Surely this isn't God; this is something else."

The more I resisted, the more my breath left my body. So I sat and silently had a dialogue with this God that was calling me. I said, "Okay God, here's your chance. If you get me down there and have this man shame and embarrass me, I'm never coming back. I won't ever trust you again. If you have him say stuff about my business over the mic, I won't trust church people again. I went on and on with God. This trip to the altar felt like the green mile. Suddenly I stood up on my feet, and it's as if God blocked everyone out of my vision, and it was just him and I. I couldn't see anyone in my peripheral, and I totally focused in on hearing this voice. I said, "Okay God, I'm heading down to you. Please, please, please, don't leave me." Tears ran down my cheeks, and the tough, hard lesbian, was beginning to lose its grip. Silently, I said a second time, "God, if you allow this man to humiliate me, I'm done with church for good."

As I got up to walk to the altar, I heard the greatest voice ever declare unto me, "Daughter it's me your Father, come to me, and I will give you rest. I will cover you and protect you. I won't embarrass you or shame you. I am here to accept you. Daughter, I love you, for you are mine. Trust me with your life, I've been waiting for you." His words choked me up, and instantly I trusted the voice and walked to the altar. The apostle immediately moved the microphone out of his hands, moved all the intercessors out of the way, and before he laid hands on me, he released a roar that shook my soul. He then whispered in my ear, prophetically he recounted my entire childhood trauma, then he declared who God had ordained me to be, and that was a prophet to the nations. He called me out of the cocoon shell and declared that I would be a butterfly and that I would rise up with beauty for ashes. At that moment, I accepted Christ as my personal savior and made the decision to walk through deliverance.

After leaving the altar I didn't know what was next, but I had never felt so free, so relieved, so light, and so joyful. This

God, who had spoken to me, was amazing. I fell in love with the prophetic, because that word shook my destiny like never before. I immediately responded to the word and prepared myself to walk with God. I was hungry and thirsty to discover that voice I heard, to discover the God, who kept his word and allowed me to be handled so graciously at the altar. I didn't know much about prayer, but I knew how to talk, so I started begging for that presence. I got so caught up chasing the voice, to the point I would be up from 9 p.m. until 4 a.m., looking for His presence. I waited on my steps for God to answer. I longed to experience what I felt in church. So every day I set a meeting place to meet God, I needed to know Him. I read the book of John and discovered that God was the word, so I looked for him in the word. I began staying up reading the gospels, and seeking God. It was a hard pursuit, and I was desperate. I was so caught up in my pursuit, that I would go days and weeks without thinking about my sexuality. I was caught up in pursuing a new interest. I wanted to become acquainted with this power. I had to know it for myself. All of a sudden my heart was set on fire, and I loved this God with all my mind, body, and soul.

I was excited to call my mother and tell her that I was saved. I couldn't wait to let her know, that I had given my life to God and that I was for real about it. My mother was excited, and she told everyone I had given my life to the Lord. I really wasn't sure what that meant. I assumed now I had to give up my habits and live a perfect life. However, God's grace and mercy were the most beautiful display of love I'd ever known. I had no idea how to be perfect. I was like a new-born baby. Lovingly, heaven nursed me. It was as if God had pulled me close to His chest, and allowed me to rest in His arms, as he nursed me from level to level. I put forth effort in chasing, craving, and longing for the voice who spoke to me before the apostle ever uttered a word. I was listening and chasing after the first voice, and then I learned to chase after the teaching and discipleship of the second voice, which was man.

I had a month before my WNBA tryout, and I was totally convinced that since I had God in my life, he would give me the desires of my heart (Psalm 37:4). I began to study the Word, and knew that there were promises in the kingdom. I learned scriptures like "knock and the door shall be open, seek and you will find, ask and you will receive." If two or more agreed upon a thing, it will be established." I mean I had the Word down pack, and I was walking in faith that my time had come, and God was going to open the door for me. So I prayed these scriptures and by faith believed them to be true in my life. I spoke to the mountains and by faith commanded them to be moved. I was ready, just a few more weeks, and I'd be well on my way.

CHAPTER 9
SAN JOSE, CALIFORNIA

$\mathcal{T}$he time had come. My big weekend in San Jose, California was finally here. I went by myself because I didn't want anyone present. I wanted to call home and announce the good news to everyone. When I was en route to California, my mom called and advised me that I was about 30 minutes away from my aunt and uncle. She expressed that she had provided them with my number and information, and stated that they would reach out to me, and plan to visit me since I was so close. I thought that was awesome, because I had such a great respect for my Aunt Debra, who is a prophetess, and for my Uncle Hodo, who is one of the greatest father's in the world. I was eager to spend time with them.

I departed to San Jose, and when I got on the plane I recognized a few other basketball players. They were dressed in sweat suits, warm-ups, gym shoes, headbands, and had basketball bags. I can recognize a ball player from a mile away. I was so excited about this time in my life. I was on the plane reading my Bible, and reminding God of his word. I felt like

I was in a good place. It was perfect timing to get saved, and I just felt like everything was working in my favor. The plane landed, and as I grabbed my bag, I took a deep breath and said to myself, the time has come. I walked inside to get my bags from checkout, and I saw a lot of ball players standing around. I wasn't scared or intimidated. I felt prepared, and with God on my side, I knew I could do it. I witnessed studs with their girlfriends, and everyone looked so happy. I didn't have a thought about no girl. I was here to finally do what I was sent in the earth to do, and that was to play the game I loved. I had my Jordan outfit on from head to toe, and I was ready to ball, hard.

We all stood outside, and a limo picked us up, and escorted us to the hotel. When we arrived, the first thing I noticed was a deaf basketball player, who was upset because she didn't' have a translator. I attempted to help her out, but she couldn't' understand much. She appreciated me trying, and we connected immediately. We checked into our rooms, and when I walked to my room, it was a huge suite with a Jacuzzi in the living room area, and an all-white robe draped over the sofa. I loved it. I felt like I was living the dream, or at least getting a sample of it. I there and gave God praise for opening the door and allowing me to live out my dream.

I spent a lot of time in my hotel room reading the Word, and delighting in God's presence. I was still newly saved, and the excitement of spending time in God's presence was my joy. I sat around the room daydreaming about me one day being drafted to the league, and becoming the new face of the WNBA. I was thinking to myself; maybe God saved me because He wanted me to be the voice that would declare to my sisters in the league that deliverance is possible. I had so many thoughts going through my head. I was getting motion sickness because the dream appeared to be so real. I was excited, and I remember saying, "Yes God, I can make it to the league, and still lift up your name." I was looking ahead at me being the comeback kid, and spreading the good news of Jesus on a national platform, while still playing the game I loved. I was focused and ready to step on the court and give it all I had.

The time had come, and it was time for me to get dressed and head to the gym. I grabbed my Nike shorts, tank top, tube socks, and J's. I put my headband, and wristband on then took my wave cap off and brushed down my waves. I was feeling great, refreshed and revived. I looked myself in the mirror, smiled and said, "The time has come." I had crazy faith to believe that today would be the day I would make my family proud and that my dream comes true. I took a deep breath, dropped to my knees and prayed. I felt confident, as I ended my prayer, blew a kiss to the heavens, and walked out the door.

The young lady I had met earlier who was deaf and couldn't hear stood outside my door and waited to walk over to the gym with me. As we walked to the gym, there were so many women from all over the world gathering in this one place. These women were of all shades, heights, weights and nationalities. I suddenly felt scared to death. My heart was racing, and I was unsure of myself. So many studs were with their feminine girlfriends, who were holding their water bottles, and standing in a cheering posture. Some of the studs were hugged up in the bleachers while waiting on registration to be complete, kissing and fondling one another in the open. The tryout looked like a gay parade, with so much sexual sin. These studs were cocky, tatted all over, and built with muscles that made my arms appear thin. I'm not going to lie; I was suddenly intimidated. I was trying to stir up my stud mentality, but it was as if I had lost my sense of power. I couldn't find the cocky Sophia, the stud, the one who could move the crowd with one word.

> *"As he walked me to the car, his voice was calm, and his words were soothing. I kicked and punched his back, saying, "How did this happen, how could God fail me. Why me? What am I supposed to do?"*

Although my appearance was very stud like, my power was stripped, and I was furious because I was looking for my dominance to arise, but nothing happened. All I could think about was God. Hold up, wait a minute God, give me a second. Not right now okay, I need my power. Calling on God felt so lame, I couldn't call on God right now and look cool in the midst of a gym full of studs. I needed to connect to the power that gave me strength, courage and personality. God was having me look around, and my heart was bleeding for so many who appeared lost and confused. I was spending time so distracted with God thoughts, and trying to tap into my inner power, that I kept drawing blanks. "God, can you please leave me alone for a second," is what I thought, but His presence was coming in like a flood. I can recall a few chics hitting on me, and making comments like, "Dang she fine, and even calling me sexy." Sexy, I felt so displaced, how can I be sexy, I'm confused. Comments of this sort usually drew me. I would usually flirt and have a good time with the ladies when they came on to me; however, I was annoyed, frustrated and bothered. They thought I had some type of attitude, but to be honest, I was uncomfortable and couldn't understand why.

I stepped outside to catch my breath and gather my thoughts. I walked under a palm tree, and sat there quietly. Suddenly two tall, athletic, very pretty feminine women came under the palm tree and asked if we could pray. Pray, wait, this must be some sort of joke. I looked at them mysteriously, and asked, "Do what?" They asked again, "Can you pray with us?" Wait, this is awkward, how do they know I'm even saved. Why are they asking me to pray, I'm over here straight struggling, and they want me to pray? So they reached for my hand, and all of a sudden I began to pray for them to perform well, play hard, put God first, and have faith that it could be done for them. I started declaring that no weapon formed against them would be able to prosper.

In the midst of the prayer, I realized I was praying for them and wasn't even including myself. They were crying and holding my hand tighter and tighter. I thought, this has got to be some type of joke. I concluded the prayer, and they gave me a hug and thanked me. One of the girls said she felt hyped up, and believed she would make the team. I was like, great. They asked how I felt, and I smiled and said, 'I'm good." They walked inside the gym, and I remained under the palm tree. Within a second of gathering my thoughts, I heard someone call my name, so I walked inside the gym and the first session of tryouts had begun. I performed well in my opinion, but it was on a whole new level. These women were aggressive. The point guards were like 5'9 and 6'0. I was short and stocky. I couldn't keep up with their aggressiveness, and was getting knocked around all over the floor. These women were from oversees and had professional experience. I laid it all on the line and left my emotions on the floor. Later that evening was the last try-out before they made cuts. Many people were getting cut tonight, and the second day was by invitation only. I played my heart out later in the evening, giving it my best. I just knew I had it, and that it was my time.

While the evening try-out was going on, I noticed a distinguished, sophisticated, tall man with glasses walk inside the gym and watch me play. I realized this man was my uncle and next to him was my auntie and their daughters. I was excited they had come out to watch me play. I hadn't seen them in years, so it was great to reunite and catch up. I was feeling proud that they had come to watch their niece achieve the very dream I had since I was a kid. At the end of the tryout, all the players were asked to sit on the floor while they called the names of those who were invited back for tomorrow's invitation only tryout. I sat with my knees up, and my head resting in my arms, wrapped around my knees. I had butterflies roaming around my stomach, and my knuckles were sweating.

They called name after name, and it appeared as if the names were in alphabetical order. When they finally got to the R's I was waiting on my name to be called. It was as if I drew a blank, and was totally out of it because I didn't hear my name. Studs were jumping up, hugging their girlfriends, kissing them, and even picking them up. I was shocked; this couldn't be happening. I didn't make it. I immediately lay on the floor and filled the gym floor with tears. I couldn't move; I literally felt a heaviness of defeat and failure overtake me. I was angry and confused. I didn't understand how I was saved, I gave God my heart, I prayed for those two girls, and they made the second round, and I was sitting here a loser.

All of my life I had prepared for this moment, and in an instant death flashed before my face. My body ached, my mind was drained, and my heart was broken. This day I left my heart on the floor and said to myself forget God, forget basketball, and forget life. As I laid on the floor in devastation, someone came and picked me up and carried me to the hotel. My uncle literally placed me over his shoulder and walked me to his car so he could take me to the hotel.

As he walked me to the car, his voice was calm, and his words were soothing. I kicked and punched his back, saying, "How did this happen, how could God fail me. Why me? What am I supposed to do?" My uncle placed me inside his van, put my seatbelt on, and drove me to the hotel. The silence in the car was defining. No one muttered a single word. My family walked me to the hotel and gave me time and space. My aunt prayed for me, but at that time, I had checked out mentally from God. I felt set up. I felt like I had trusted this God, and he had stripped me of my power at the time I needed it most. My family departed, and my plan set in. Suicide was my only option. I called my mom, and I called Devon screaming, "I didn't make it." I then hung up on them not giving them a chance to respond. I was ready to end this life; there was nothing else for me to do.

"The game has suddenly changed for you daughter. I had a plan for you before the foundations of the world, and it can't be altered or reversed. Before I formed you in your mother's womb I separated you and set you apart, consecrating you and ordaining you to be a prophet to the nations."

I climbed into the Jacuzzi, leaned my head back, and closed my eyes. I had never thought about suicide ever until this day. It wasn't even a thought; it was a plan, and I was ready to execute. I whispered to God, "Why did you let me down? Why? How could you set me up like this, only to wound me and hurt me?" I was ashamed, embarrassed and didn't know what to do with my life. I took the scriptures at face value, and I believed, but nothing came to pass for me. I don't trust the word, these words are lies, and I began quoting back scripture reminding God that he said if I had faith,

I could move mountains if I touched and agreed on anything it would come to pass.

I was confused, I was angry, and I had a flashback of my entire life. "Why," was all I asked. "Why would you bring me this far, then leave me? How could you strip me of my power and openly shame me? How can I return to my family and friends telling them I'm a failure, and that I didn't make it? What am I supposed to do now, after all, this was the only life I knew? I don't have any other passions or love; basketball is my love. Why would you have me pray for those girls, and they both make the second round, and the one who prayed goes home. This doesn't make any sense. You failed me, God. All my life I lived, and prepared for this moment. I spent countless hours sowing into my destiny, and this is what I reap, failure?"

In the midst of me complaining, I heard a voice so strong, so confirming and so convincing say, "Sophia you may as well kill yourself. You may as well die. Surely there is nothing good coming out of your life. You are a failure, a great big disappointment. And this God you called upon never loved you, He's angry with you. You thought serving HIM would cause your dreams to come true. Well look at him, he failed you again. He's the reason you're gay. He's the reason your father walked out on you. He's' the reason your family talks about you. He's the reason you were abused, abandoned and neglected. This God could care less about you. Don't worry about telling anyone you love them, none of those people loved you. You were robbed of your childhood, and you thought you were going to be some type of savior. Well, you can forget that. Look at how much he loved those beautiful girls you prayed for. Look at them; they are rewarded and once again you're the face of a joke. Just die Sophia, kill yourself. No one will even realize you're gone. End your life, just sink down in this water, and within a few minutes, you will be forgotten about. This hard life will be over, and you can rest from this life."

As my body began to sink slowly, and my chin hit the water, I could feel my body stiffen. I got scared and came back up. I went down again and put my face under the water, but I was holding my breath. The voice said, "Don't hold your breath, open your mouth, and in a few minutes, you will be gone." As soon as my head hit the water, my nose infused with water, and I heard another voice. This voice captured my attention, and I felt a sense of security and strength. This voice declared, "The game has suddenly changed for you daughter. I had a plan for you before the foundations of the world, and it can't be altered or reversed. Before I formed you in your mother's womb I separated you and set you apart, consecrating you and ordaining you to be a prophet to the nations. I call you unto myself. You are mine, and I am yours. I am a jealous lover over your soul, and the time has come for me to bring you closer to me. You had a plan, but my plan prevails. I called you my child; you are my beloved in whom I'm well pleased. I'm going to use your story. Fear not for you are not only a child; you are a prophet to the nations. You are the comeback kid, and I will use you to snatch others out of the fire. You are a game changer, and I allowed you to rise in the arena of sports and allowed you to comprehend the role of a point guard, so you would understand the function of a prophet. You learned submission early; you learned leadership, and you grasp the concept of a coach-player relationship. You learned to drown out the noises of distractions, and you have proven yourself to have a loyal heart of love.

Now is the time I change the game, and I will now give you the desires of MY heart. Will your burning desire be for me, daughter? Will you go for me, daughter? Will you rise and be my ambassador in the earth? I am your coach, and I shall personally orchestrate my plans through you. I will now give you access to the kingdom, and will release my words to you. You shall go out before all the nations and announce my words over the earth. You shall speak from the embassy of heaven, and I will reveal my heart to you. I will take you places basketball couldn't take you, and I will cause you to pioneer a brand new move. Rise up Sophia it's now your time, And I shall give you strength to not only slay the Goliath of homosexuality, but you shall cut off the head, and take the sword. Come back, go forth throughout the earth and share the goodness of Jesus. I am with you every step of the way. Vengeance is mine says the Lord, and hell will pay the price for touching my very elect. Fear not for I am with you." I jumped out of the Jacuzzi, tears flowing down my face, and I felt a sense of freedom. I felt relief, and I felt so secure. I didn't have a clue what God meant, but once again

I longed to chase after the voice that had just saved my life. I got dressed, sat on the couch and began reading my Bible.

Suddenly I heard a knock at my door, so I looked through the peephole. The deaf girl was at my door, and she asked if she could come inside. I opened the door and signaled for her to come in. She came inside and sat on my couch. I didn't know how to communicate with her because she was deaf, so she just sat and looked at me. I was confused on what to do, so I got a piece of paper and a pen for her to write down what she needed. While she was writing, I walked into my room for a second to grab something. While in my room, I heard that same voice that had spoken to me earlier say, "Daughter pray for her. She's angry with me, and I want to use you right now to pray for her. Trust me, and do as I instruct you." I said,

"Lord why is she angry with you?" I assumed she was angry because she hadn't made the team, and maybe she felt how I felt. Then the voice said, "She's angry because in the Word (the Bible), the word dumb is a stumbling block. She doesn't understand why the spirit is called deaf and dumb, but pray for her, and I will give you the words you are to pray."

The voice said, "Just open your mouth wide and I'm going to fill it. I walked back into the living room, and the young lady had my Bible open and was aggressively pointing at the word dumb. She then wrote all over the paper deaf and dumb, deaf and dumb. She asked the question with tears rolling down her face, "Why am I called dumb by God?". I had no clue how to answer her question. I had no experience in this field, so I trusted that God would answer her once I opened my mouth. Then I thought to myself, how can she hear my prayers if she's deaf, and the Lord said, "She shall receive and be changed." I began praying and even laid my hands on her ears. The more I prayed, the more the tears flowed down her face. Her hands went up slowly, and she shook her head up and down. I was amazed, but I was unsure of what was happening. After prayer, she gave me a hug, left her email address, and walked out of my room. I sat there stunned and clueless, but it felt so good to be a part of blessing someone.

As I prepared to depart from San Jose, the voice reminded me, "Well done Sophia, I told you, this wasn't a tryout for you, you're already on the team. My team.."

CHAPTER 10
HOMOSEXUALITY LOST ITS GRIP

Now that my altar call experience was over, I was back in the real world, and out of my supernatural bubble. What's next? What happens after the altar?

J learned very quickly that every morning my appetites were still calling my name. My hunger was starving, and in my own strength, I had no clue how not to respond to the cravings I longed for. It was like I was on some type of spiritual diet, where I was trying to deny myself access to the unhealthy perversions that I was so used to indulging in on a daily basis. Whenever I felt the craving, I responded. The cravings never stopped. If I was to be honest, the cravings intensified. I didn't have a clue about what to do with all these urges. So I responded, " Now what God! I didn't call you, but you called me Lord, and I'm really clueless on how to deny my flesh from the very things it's seeking." I knew it was impossible for me to put an end to my life on my own, so I learned quickly to turn to God. Although I had a strong spiritual father who assisted in my walk towards deliverance, I discovered the wonders of making a covenant with God himself. I didn't want the mantle of Elijah; I wanted the full measure, an outpouring of the full manifestation of the 7-fold Holy Spirit. Quickly, Romans chapter 8, became the scriptures I ate and digested daily. There is therefore no condemnation for those who are called.

I never once attempted to alter my personality, change my style or rush my process. I submitted to God, and my submission gave me power and authority to resist the devil and make him flee. I was hungry for God, and I knew that in spite of my worldly desires, I had to burn for God. I wanted to be a consuming fire. I wanted to want God because I wanted to. I wanted to recklessly abandon my life to pursue holiness. Holiness wasn't religion for me; holiness was my life. I wanted to look like God, burn like God, and cultivate back to my original state, and that was to see myself in His image. I was training my thoughts, and fixing my gaze on the new lover of my soul that had invaded my space, and refused to compete with any other love. I learned to stir and awaken a love that I was willing to satisfy. In order for me to launch into this love, I had to become acquainted with the lover of my soul. God wanted all of me, so he took His time driving out my enemies little by little.

Because I was a stud, and I had an outer exterior that didn't define my original nature, God spent years dealing with what mattered most, and that was my internal structure.

God invaded my internal being by taking his Holy hands and supernaturally dusting the webs off of my heart. He broke down the walls that were around my heart by tearing down, and breaking the chains that were wrapped around my heart. God unlocked me from hurt, guilt, shame, abuse, rejection, trauma and hatred. He cracked the demonic code that had been set against my heart over the years and entered a new passcode that spelled agape. I felt a change in my heart. The Messiah was healing the numbness that I had experienced for years.

Once my heart was released and free, God brought fire from the throne room, and as a wick, he lit the tip of my heart, which burned with a reverence, a love and a passion that would lead me to pursue him like never before. I was burning for Jesus. Oh, how I was spinning out of control, with a love language that spoke, "God you are the lover of my soul. I began to declare Lord, I vow to love you, I yearn for you, and I spill over with adoration for you. I didn't desire anything materialistic anymore. I was past making requests. I just wanted to gaze into the eyes of the King, who had rescued me from the powers of darkness that tried to destroy me eternally. I was finally free in my heart and was able to recognize the love of a father, and the love of a lover.

After undressing my heart, God put coals upon my lips, and the taste was sweeter than honey. I was craving for the word that was sweeter than honey. I desired and hungered for the taste of His words. My taste buds were altered. I began to learn the difference between good and evil. Evil had a taste that was bitter, and when I went towards evil, I would be reminded of the good taste of my father. God began to spoon feed me with His Word, and I thirsted for the refreshing water of the Spirit. God then baptized my mind by giving me the mind of Christ. He placed a helmet of salvation upon my head. I learned to literally bring my thoughts into captivity. God invaded the demonic playground of my imagination by uprooting perverted images and thoughts. God dug up those images from the root and planted His spermatic seeds in my mind that overtook every negative word and thought. God changed the tape and sang a new song over me. Songs of deliverance, and songs of love played over and over in my heart and in my mind until I sang them aloud and those words became life. God dealt with my senses, all five of them.

My eye gate was fixed on Jesus. I could see again, and I was able to see myself as God sees me. I saw beauty even in the midst of my appearance outwardly not being changed. I saw beauty like never before. My ear gate was adjusted, and I began to hear the very whispers of the Lord that drove out every negative word of the enemy. I recognized the sound of God from the sound of the enemy. My nose gate was altered. I began to smell the very fragrance of holiness. God perfumed with his purity and cleanliness produced a beautiful aroma. My nostrils drew towards the smell of holiness, and immediately I was able to smell evil and wickedness. I could smell the very things that were a stench to my father's nostrils. My mouth gate was watered with the desires of taking in the goodness of Jesus. Once my eyes, ears, nose, and mouth were changed, my sense of touch shifted. I touched pure and holy things. Whenever my hands attempted to touch evil, I could feel it and know that it wasn't God. When the Lord declared to Samuel that he doesn't judge by man's outer experience, but by the internal man, that is exactly how God dealt with me.

"I began to move in power and command demons to flee. I fought the good fight of faith, and recognized my warfare was not with flesh and blood. I fought for my deliverance by remaining submitted and accountable."

To be honest, I was confused on how God was more concerned with my inner being than he was with my external. I mean it was difficult walking this lifestyle out still looking like a dude, but full of God internally. Don't get me wrong, when God was dealing with me internally, it wasn't an easy process, it was a submitted process. I submitted myself to God for real, for real, in real life. One thing about my personality is, if I'm with you, I'm with you. When I decided to give my life to God, I was true about it, and desired to be all I could be in God. I refused to be out of the closet while I was in a homosexual lifestyle only to be in the closet in church. There was no way, so behind the scenes, I sought God and gave myself away.

Submission is key in order to walk through your deliverance. You must submit to God before you can ever get to the

...nension of resisting the devil. Without submission, you can't resist your human natures, cravings or appetites. I never tried to stop my addictions cold turkey, because I knew that just as I stopped them on my own, there was room for them to return seven times worse. So submission, holding God to his word, and knowing that I didn't call Him, but he chose me, is what I rested in. I rested in the fact that if I submitted myself to him, he would do the hard part by dealing with the enemies that were too hard for me. Homosexuality no longer was my fight, this battle was not mines, it belonged to the Lord.

Submission to God is key, and accountability to leadership is mandatory during your journey of deliverance. I was accountable to my spiritual father, and he was responsible for watching over my soul. He governed me during my process of deliverance by seeing who I was and not focusing on who I am. Now because I was still a stud outwardly, it was difficult for one to discern what God was doing in my life, and I was often mishandled by the church. People would wonder if I was really saved, and if I was really walking through deliverance how could this be when nothing outwardly demonstrated any form of manifestation.

The pressure of the church was intense. If I had not made a covenant with God, the church would have crucified me. The apostle was under great pressure, people were making threats to leave the church, and key leaders discussed and staffed me on a weekly basis like I was some type of mental health patient. The same members who cheered on my process, were reviewing my process and crucifying me behind the scenes. They couldn't understand the timing of God, and they had no idea what me and God were doing behind closed doors. It took the man of God to risk his reputation and his ministry to believe that God had a plan for my life, and that behind the mask of a stud was a prophet to the nations. People were weighing my deliverance on my outward appearance, but God hadn't touched the outward man. He was making covenant with my inward being. I was under construction internally, and I couldn't say a word. I was accountable from the moment I left the altar. I attended church weekly. I was one of the first to arrive for 5 a.m. prayer. I was at Bible Study. I got there early and stayed late talking and taking in everything I needed to know. I had a notebook to take notes as I sat with my eyes fixed on the man of God as he preached, and I longed to receive the impartation that was being released. I paid my tithes; I sowed seeds on a consistent basis, and at one point I challenged myself in my giving by sowing 15 percent instead of 10. I was determined, and I didn't miss a beat. I surrounded myself with leadership and spent time asking questions, seeking answers, and desiring the prophetic like never before.

There were so many times while walking through deliverance that I was killed between the porch and the altar. The same voices that spoke in tongues, prophesied and cast out devils, were the same voices that were backbiting, eye rolling, and pressuring the apostle to do something about me. God allowed me to see it all, and He said to endure the pressure, for I am going to make your enemies your footstool. I endured the pressure because I knew that God was doing something in me, and soon the world would know.

Many outsiders questioned my deliverance and to be honest I questioned it too. Women would still hit on me and make advances, because of my outward appearance. When I would say I was in church or had a relationship with God, they would ask, "How is that possible, when you look like a dude?" Those words crushed me to the core, but I wasn't going to allow the pressure of man to cause me to miss my divine appointments. I asked God why he was waiting to change me outwardly, and the Lord declared, "Daughter before you manifested outwardly as a stud, you designed an inward blueprint of who you wanted to become, so I must redefine you inwardly, and soon I will unzip you outwardly." God continued to remind me that this battle was not mine, but it belonged to him. So I continued the process.

In the beginning, I fell weekly to sexual sin, then I would go months, and finally I was able to go an entire year clean and sober from sexual sin. Each time I fell, I got right back up and bounced back. I repented and presented my body to God. I was transparent and honest by telling God about my struggles. I took responsibility. I didn't hide or cover my sin. I exposed it to God and cried out for help. I flexed my spiritual muscles and became stronger and stronger with resisting the devil. I began to move in power and command demons to flee. I fought the good fight of faith, and recognized my warfare was not with flesh and blood. I fought for my deliverance by remaining submitted and accountable. I took the initiative to learn about deliverance. I purchased Pigs In A Parlor and learned to do self-deliverance. I exercised my spiritual gift and continued to strive for holiness. When I would get down on myself, God would bring scripture to my remembrance. I learned how to be pro-active against the enemy, and scattered them before they could take me out.

One day I was listening to Lil Wayne, and I was spitting harder than Wheezy F baby, please say the baby. I was headed to the car wash, windows down, fresh breeze blowing in my face, and the smell of a good day blooming. I turned into the carwash, and I heard this voice say, "Throw away all your CD's and put on some Martha Munnizi." I laughed and thought I was going too far with the God stuff. Then I heard it again, and without hesitation, I threw away an entire collection of CDs. I then went to the Christian bookstore to purchase Shirley Caesar, and a friend of mine gave me Martha Munizzi. From that day forward, my ear gate was closed to secular music, and I never looked back.

Over time, the Lord began instructing me to get rid of specific things. At this point, I never questioned his voice because I knew it. The Lord had me get rid of all sexual objects, and he completely stripped me of the things that made me feel empowered and masculine. He took away a piece of my manhood, so I thought. Slowly but surely homosexuality was losing its grip. I was being wiped clean of the enemy's influence and his power. At last, Sophia was being refined and redefined. Obedience is better than sacrifice. I had to obey in order to fully walk out my deliverance. I had to obey the voice of God; which triumphed over the voice of man. The enemy was getting weaker, and I was gaining momentum. Once I stripped myself of my masculine sexual objects, I never purchased anything else. It was a wrap.

After that, it became difficult to imagine me sexually active again. For me, the game had completely changed. I quit the club scene immediately. I didn't have to change friends, they changed on me, and walked away. My language changed. I wasn't intentional, but my only conversation was on what was current in my life, and that was God.

Then this Happened:

While visiting my family in Chicago we decided to attend church for worship. I was down for it, because I was in love with God and wanted to be in his presence. I had grown my hair out and had braids. I was still rocking baggy clothes and Timberland boots. Nothing about my appearance changed other than my hair. It was braided, and instead of slicing both eyebrows, only one was sliced. My family knew my heart was on fire and they were accepting of my walk with Christ. They never rushed my process or pressed me to change, they just enjoyed watching me grow in God. My excitement was full, and every day I would call my family to testify about what God was doing in my life. One evening, my mother, my sister and my brother-in-law all departed my mom's home and went into the church. We worshipped and prayed our hearts out. We sang and lifted up the name of Jesus.

Now if any of you know my mother, you know she's not one to say much unless she's truly led by God. So my mother suddenly turned towards me, and with a look of power she stared at me and began to proclaim "Prophetess, prophetess, prophetess, come forth, prophetess come forth." She got louder and louder, coming closer and closer to me. I hit the floor in tears and confusion wondering what was going on. "What is a prophetess," I wondered. So I left it in God's hands and enjoyed the amazing feeling of relief and strength my mother had just released. My mother prophetically called me forth and that was the beginning of a new move in my walk. I returned home, and the entire train ride, I kept hearing the my mother saying, "Prophetess, come forth." Wow, what a feeling. I felt so good about myself and my new life in Christ.. When I arrived back home, I studied on the prophetic, and began wanting to learn more about a prophetess.

This is when things got interesting. A few months after visiting with my family, I shared with Devon that I wanted to surprise my mother for Mother's Day. Devon asked me what I wanted to do, and I said, "I want to dress like a girl for my mother." I said, " Now Devon I'm only doing this one time, so I can put a smile on my mother's face. I want to reward her for being such an amazing mother during my journey of deliverance. My mother never turned her back on me, never bad mouthed me, and never rejected me. She was a praying mother, and she loved me with a love beyond words. So I told Devon I needed her help with making this one of the greatest moments of my mother's life. I wanted to be the greatest gift she had had in years, to finally see her daughter dressed like a girl after years of masculinity. Devon seemed super excited and said, " Absolutely Sophia, that would be awesome."

Devon and I went to the mall to shop for an outfit. While shopping, I was embarrassed because I had never shopped in the women's section. I didn't know my size, and I didn't even know how to put the clothes against my body to determine if something looked right. It was weird being in the store because the workers recognized me from shopping in the men's section all the time. I pretended to be with Devon and allowed her to pick out the outfit, and I told her I would try them on later. Devon shopped away, as multiple people came inside the store saying, "Hey Sophia, how y'all doing?" I was so embarrassed, and all I could think is, "What am I getting myself into?" Devon played it off so graciously. She held the clothes in her hand and asked me my opinion, acting as we were shopping together. I was sweating bullets from embarrassment.

Once Devon picked the outfit, we both went to the dressing room. I was ashamed because I didn't want anyone to see me trying on girl's clothes. I mean I was looking like a dude, yet I was in the dressing room trying on Capri pants and feminine shirts. I felt weird, but I was determined to bless my mother for Mother's Day. I walked into the dressing room, and I had Devon hand me the clothes. I literally tried on everything with my eyes closed, and trusted that if

I could fit it, it would be perfect to wear. I didn't care what I had on, I just needed something girly. Devon purchased the outfit and carried the bags out of the store. She then went to buy me some jewelry and underwear. I had been so used to wearing boxers and men's underwear that I had no clue what size I needed in panties or a bra.

> *"I ran into my mother's arms, and she wept over me. Her heart was relieved, and she continued to say, "Baby, my baby Sophia, you are so beautiful. My baby, my baby." That moment was one of the most powerful mother-daughter encounters I ever experienced."*

So Devon assisted me with this moment, and it was beautiful from start to finish. Finally, she said, "Sophia, how about we go to the beautician to see if she would flat iron your hair." I said, " Oh no, I'm not going inside no shop, and all those women looking at me getting my hair done." Devon and I went to the shop to see if anyone was inside. When we arrived, no one was there, and the stylist agreed to lock the shop, bring me inside and do my hair. This young lady did my hair, and when she went put the mirror in my face, I covered my face, and didn't want to see myself. I kept saying, " This is only for my mother, not for me." I couldn't stomach seeing me in any other form than what I was accustomed to.

The stylist immediately wrapped my hair, and I tied a black do-rag on my head. I had no clue what I looked like, but I was all set for my trip home for the holiday. I called my sister and brother-in-law to advise them of my plan. They were excited and said my mother was going to love this surprise. My mother had no idea I was even coming home. My brother-in-law and sister picked me up from the train station at 8 a.m. Mother's Day morning. They dropped me off at my mom's friend's home, Betty Mo, where I was to get dressed and ride with her to church to surprise my mother.

I showered and prepared myself to get ready. I ironed my clothes, laid them on the bed and laughed at what I was about to put on. This was the only outfit I had. My entire suitcase was filled with my usual garments. Boxers, shorts, big shirts, and Jordan's, and I had a hat to pull my hair in a ponytail and put my hat on, as soon as church was over. I got dressed, then I took a comb and let down my hair. I sat on the bed and called Devon, telling her that I was dressed and I was about to head out for church. Devon asked how I looked, and at that moment I had no clue what I looked like.

As I was talking, I walked passed a mirror and accidentally ran into myself. Immediately tears burst down my cheeks. I couldn't stop crying; something broke inside of me. I couldn't resist the tears, and Devon was on the phone asking, "Sophia are you okay, Sophia are you there?" I cried out, "Oh my gosh Devon; this is me. I look so beautiful. Wow, look at me." I hung up the phone and walked closer to the mirror. Immediately the voice of God said, "Look at my beloved, in whom I'm well pleased. My daughter, in my image, after my likeness. My Sophia Ruffin, oh how beautiful you are to behold, for today I give you beauty for ashes. My butterfly can now soar." I was undone. Betty was calling my name, and I couldn't move. I was stunned. I walked down the stairs, and Betty began to cry, and continued to say, "Your mom is going to be so happy Sophia. Oh, how beautiful you are young lady."

We arrived at the church, and my mother was already in the choir stand singing. I walked inside and sat with my nieces and nephews. They hugged me, and couldn't stop saying, "Auntie you're so beautiful. Auntie, look at you." They were touching my face and kissing my cheeks. My sister grabbed my hand and held it with a look of admiration. My brother-in-law looked over, nodded his head and smiled. My nephew, who was on the drums, smiled so hard at his auntie and beat the drums like a wild child. My mother then looked at her friend. She had a look of confusion. Her lips were mumbling, but I couldn't make out the words, as she shrugged her shoulders, and shook her head as if she couldn't make out who I was. She then asked, "Who is that lady with my family? What is she doing? What's all the commotion about?" My mother continued to stare with a look of mysteriousness. I waved at my mom, wondering why she hadn't responded. My mother shrugged her shoulders and continued to look confused.

Finally, someone said, "Doris that's your daughter." My mother covered her mouth, her eyes enlarged, and she stood up with her arms reaching for me to come and hug her. The pastor halted the service and allowed us to have a moment. I ran into my mother's arms, and she wept over me. Her heart was relieved, and she continued to say, "Baby, my baby Sophia, you are so beautiful. My baby, my baby." That moment was one of the most powerful mother-daughter encounters I ever experienced. The very fact that my mother saw no residue, and couldn't recognize her own child, was a clear indication that my deliverance was full term.

At the end of service, we went home, and everyone talked about that moment. I was so happy to be a part of bringing my mother so much joy. When it was time to undress, I tried to put on my clothes, and I couldn't fit into them. I couldn't put them on. I had no power to put any of those garments on. I called Devon and said, " Devon I don't know what to do." I explained that I had no other outfits and that I couldn't put on any of the garment I had brought. I said to God, "What am I going to do because I didn't have anything else." I wore that same outfit for three days until I made it back to Mt. Vernon. The Lord spoke and said, " My garments are now changed. He had given me beauty for ashes; old things had passed away and everything from this day forward was new." I wept and wept. I felt a ripping in my soul. I was separated from the lifestyle of homosexuality. The spirit lost its grip and had to let me go. When I arrived back home, Devon had seven new feminine outfits for me, and I got rid of my entire wardrobe, leaving nothing to be remembered. I've never gone back. My entire being was forever changed. My wardrobe was made new.

Once I was no longer a stud, homosexuality lost its entire grip. My personality, demeanor, attitude and everything that gripped me to same-sex perversion was destroyed. The connection was gone. The last time I attempted to engage sexually, in the midst of the act, I felt the heart of God and broke down weeping in the middle of the act. I wept and from that point on, I have been clean and sober, no setbacks, no looking back. No longer was my appetite yearning for the same-sex. I was released to walk in sexual purity, and I experienced the full measure of deliverance.

Homosexuality had become my Goliath, and this enemy tormented me for years. This enemy taunted my bloodline and terrorized my family. Every day this enemy challenged me and declared I would never be free. This enemy appeared impossible to be destroyed. Homosexuality is a spirit many are afraid to confront. Even leaders are intimidated by this spirit, and refuse to engage war against it. After slaying this Goliath, I cut the head and took the sword. Now I am a champion, and I cut the head of the very enemy that tormented my family, never to be seen again. There is a Davidic anointing released upon the sons and daughters of Yahweh to rise up and take the head of your enemies. Once you cut the head of your enemy, take the sword, and walk boldly into Victory. I have the head and the sword...Hallelujah.

HOMOSEXUALITY LOST ITS GRIP!!!!

CHAPTER 11
FROM POINT GUARD TO PROPHET

$\mathcal{N}$ow that homosexuality had lost its grip, the making of a prophet began. The Lord informed me that my role of a point guard was a guide to teach me the function of a prophet. As a point guard, the number one thing I had to master was the coach-player relationship. Regardless of my gift, or how good I was, if I didn't have a solid relationship with my coach, I wouldn't be effective. Point guards have to be teachable and open to correction. The weight of victory and losses is the point guard's responsibility. The point guard must be able to respond quickly to change, make adjustments in the midst of pressure, and hear the sound of the coach when the room is loud and chaotic. The point guard should anticipate what the coach is about to say before the coach even speaks. The point guard must have the ability to know the heart of the coach, and the ability to execute even in the absence of the coach. The point guard is responsible for leading the team, encouraging the team, and responding under pressure. They should also be able to handle adversity without panicking, have the skill to make others better, and be the floor general, the decision maker, and the person who's capable of handling the ball and making critical decisions even when exhausted. Point guards are triple threats, able to shoot from long or short range, playmakers, making plays at all times, crossing over opponents, making triple threat moves, and able to control the tempo and pace of the game. Point guards want the ball in their hands when the game is on the line, they dive for loose balls, they win hustle plays, and they take pride in their assist to turnover ratio. Point guards don't mind getting in the face of their teammates, and instructing them on what to do, how to do it, and when to do it. The point guard carries the heart of the team, and is responsible for both victories and losses.

While training for the WNBA, I woke up at 2 a.m. to make it to training at 3 a.m. I trained from 3 a.m. until 5 a.m. I worked out intensely and conditioned privately before everyone else. I took pride in my private practice, so that when it was time to practice as a team, I was already mentally, physically and emotionally strong. These are some of the responsibilities I had as a point guard. The Lord allowed me to keep my point guard mentality in the realm of the spirit, and as a prophet, I am responsible for the same functions. Although the responsibility is so much greater, these are only a few of the skills I developed.

Accepting my call as a prophet to the nations, I discovered similar strategies in the realm of the spirit. I developed a longing to hear and obey my coach, which is the Holy

Spirit. I had to learn how to connect with the Father, and being an ambassador sent from the Embassy of Heaven, I had to learn to execute his will in the earth. I learned not to respond to the sounds that were going off simultaneously. I wasn't dismayed at their faces whether they cheered me on or booed me. I had to press past the noise, and key into the mind and heart of the Father. I had to be coachable and willing to learn, even being rebuked. In the midst of ministering and going forth, I learned to develop a sensitivity to the spirit, and to make adjustments as necessary, according to the flow of the service. I am responsible for leading my team to advance the kingdom; I must respond under pressure, despite the noise of the enemy and demonic resistance. I have to be a floor general, a decision maker, and capable of setting my own atmosphere. I have to have the skill to usher in the presence, even when others are not feeling the anointing.

I am responsible for controlling the pace and tempo of the service when necessary, knowing how to tap into the rivers of living water, and move in grace as the spirit gives utterance. I learned to cross over demonic opposition, to be a triple threat against the enemy in my devotional life, fasting life, prayer life, and worship life. I am responsible for training, studying, showing myself approved and ministering before the Lord in private before doing so in public. I am responsible for creating space to score on the enemy, being pro-active, being offensive minded, and able to defend when necessary. I must learn to how to carry the presence of the Lord graciously, making sure I am mentally, physically, emotionally and spiritually stable at all times. I am responsible for exhortation, edifying and providing comfort when I minister; and speaking life even when my back is against the wall. Prophets have a will to win, are vocal leaders, and are sensitive to the spirit. Prophets take the hits, they are crowned at one moment and crucified when they make a mistake. Prophets have stamina, endurance, persistence, and a desire to see God's kingdom executed in the earth. Prophets will go the extra mile, they will take the hard shots, and they will do what others refuse to do. Prophets are willing to maneuver through adversity and have a desire to see an entire nation changed for the glory of God.

My Preparation Prayer Before Game Time

Lace up Sophia! You ready, it's game time. Coach, what plays are you are calling today? Team get ready, I need my angels on post, may every position be filled with your presence Lord. Execution time, game time. Apply oil to my muscles, and give me flexibility and versatility to implement your plan tonight. Lord, you've studied the opponents, you know what we are up against, now give me the plays that I may execute every play strategically. Game time. I hear you Lord, put the opportunity in my hand, I want to advance the kingdom. Give me floor vision to see! Let us set the tempo and pace of the game. Scoreboard check, I prophesy numerous victories, and multiple souls brought forth. Let's get it Holy Spirit. Stand strong Holy Spirit, and dictate the flow of the game. Silence the crowds, and let me hear the volume of your voice. Okay, I'm ready, I'm hyped. I'm stirred up and ready to roar. Time for the armor to be applied. Release your truth, release the breastplate of righteousness, come on feet get ready for the preparation of the gospel of peace. Shield of faith I grab hold of you, and we will quench all fiery darts of the wicked, put on your helmet of salvation, and pick up the sword of the Spirit, which is the word of God. Let's go Holy Ghost; it's game time!

CHAPTER 12
HOW TO MINISTER TO A HOMOSEXUAL

*M*inistering to a homosexual takes skill, grace, authority and a clear understanding of your jurisdiction. So many times people in the church world looked at me like I was a science project. Homosexuals are not a hypothesis where one takes an educated guess to figure out how to solve the problem. When dealing with homosexuality, you must center your focus around the root issues, due to homosexuality being an outward behavior that originates from rooted issues like rejection, abandonment, molestation, neglect and trauma, to name a few. You can't just walk up to a homosexual tongue talking and expecting to see results. Wisdom is the principle thing, and establishing a relationship is key to see progress. Depending on how far they are into the lifestyle, homosexuals have their own culture. You need to take the time to understand their language, get background information, and study the culture before walking up to someone and expecting them to change because you are coming in the name of Jesus with no power. Here's an example of what I mean.

If you were to visit a foreign country, and you had no idea where you were going and what you were about to get yourself into, you would spend time researching and gathering some understanding of where you were headed. You wouldn't just fly to the nations, without first assessing the environment, understanding the language, establishing some form of relationship, and being aware of what they eat, what offends them and how they respond. You will have spent time diligently researching and preparing yourself before the trip. That's the same way it should be before you step out to evangelize or disciple a homosexual.

Homosexuals, especially those in the transgender community, have established their own culture, and if you're not careful, your approach can offend them before you get the word God out of your mouth. The approach is critical. Not that you should walk on egg shells, but the fact is that you're dealing with a strong spirit that's bound by a spirit of rejection, self-rejection, pride, fear of man, delusions, and distortions. You want to be sensitive to the Spirit, and know what you're up against. Homosexuals feel justified in their sexuality, and they look for justice in every situation. Because they have been violated, deprived, neglected, abandoned and traumatized, they feel that they are justified in their sexuality. Many believe they were born this way, and if you say the wrong thing like, "God wants to help you with your 'struggle,'" or if you mention anything about them knowing they're sinning and going to hell, they will shut down, and you can forget about gaining entrance. All homosexuals do not hate

God, so let's get rid of that myth. What they despise are hypocrites, who come to them out of a false assignment, with condemning messages and no demonstration.

When you have jurisdiction, you have authority, authorization, and are endorsed by heaven to deal with the spirit of homosexuality. You have apostolic authority to engage war against the power of darkness, and the demons will come under your subjection. When you are "sent" to minister to a homosexual, you are not going with a premeditated plan on how you believe the deliverance will take place. You are going with discernment, skill, knowledge and understanding on how to speak to power. Spend time talking to the homosexual, get to know the person, not the sin.

Once you spend enough time establishing a relationship and gaining respect, they will become vulnerable and open to receive from you. Don't be deep and religious, tongue talking and moving off false inspiration. Be led by God, and obey Him as he gives you the exact words to say to break down the powers of darkness, and unleash His power. Don't use your platform to condemn and do a hate speech, speak love, speak power, speak the blood, and the power of resurrection, and allow God to convict their hearts and overturn demonic verdicts. Step out of your opinion, and go into the spirit for instructions on how to minister to the homosexual assigned to you. If the person isn't assigned to your jurisdiction stay in your lane, and allow God to send the sent one to minister to that particular person. Remember everyone isn't your assignment.

If it's a loved one, a son, daughter, or family member, don't use family functions, to bash and reject them. Don't use gatherings to make them the center of your conversation. Don't point out the homosexual, but leave the liar, adulterer, fornicator and drug addict alone. If you're going to address sin, address sin in its entirety. Don't call the pastor over to double team your child by pouring oil on his or her head, while screaming come out. You must know what you're commanding, what are you expelling.

Parents love your child, hate the sin. Embrace your baby, by having the anointing of Hannah and presenting that child back to God. Remind God that before your child was yours, that child belonged to Him, and trust that God will remember the plan He had for your child before lending him or her to you. Don't give up on your child. No matter how far gone, they may appear, for the Lord has a plan for every person that comes into the earth.

Prophecy, speak over your child and declare the plan of God for their destiny. The more you reject your child, the further you push them into the arms of their lover. Ask God for wisdom, for strategy and for understanding. Talk to your child and find out how they are doing as a person, and re-establish relationship, until your child opens up and releases what is going on in their life. Go to war secretly for your child. Consecrate yourself, and watch how God will break the powers off your child. Parents minister to the Lord in secret, and trust that He will openly reward you with the deliverance of your seed.

Homosexuals are human beings. They have been deprived of healthy and appropriate love, protection, nurturance, validation, and affirmation. Behind the mask of their delusion is a little girl or little boy that was traumatized and is seeking love. Be careful how you respond and handle a homosexual. Don't judge a book by its cover because they may just be the next prophet to the nations.

PRAYERS

Father, I lift up every parent who's grieving for their son or daughter who's bound by the spirit of homosexuality. I come against the spirit of guilt, shame, and condemnation. I break the spirit that says it's my fault, what did I do wrong, where did I fail my child. The spirit of blame I command you to flee in Jesus name. I come against every lie of the enemy, every spirit of deception and shame. I break division, discord, and disunity that pushes parents away from the child, and the child away from the parents. I release the blood between the wedges of division and command that the blood will break through the intensity of demonic warfare waging against families due to the invasion of homosexuality. I break the spirit of bitterness and unforgiveness that will make the child hate the parent, and have a hardness of heart, stemming from resentment. I break false pressures put on parents by church members and family members that are pressuring them to reject their seed. I prophesy that parents will rise up with the anointing of Hannah and will present their child back to the king. I prophesy unity and oneness.

I declare wholeness and a reuniting season for parents and children. I prophesy that the parents voice will arise in this hour, and they will decree and declare liberty for the captives. I prophesy that you Lord will massage the broken hearts, and will release healing, deliverance, and restoration. I prophesy strength to the weak and feeble parent that's ready to throw in the towel. May the grace be upon them to see that child as you see the child Lord. I declare a reuniting of the protocols in this hour.

Father, I thank you that you're moving upon every person enslaved by the spirit of homosexuality. I thank you that your power is going forth, and your word is cutting and ripping through the power of darkness. I speak to the strongman of deception that will have one believe right is wrong and wrong is right. I prophesy that your voice is at the right place, at the right time, saying the right stuff that will minister to the homosexual and they will be as Saul by running into power. I declare that the ministers, the sent ones, will rise up and go into uncommon places to announce your glory. I prophesy that this will be the year of response from the homosexual community. I break rejection, pride, abandonment and trauma off their lives. Release your arrows of flame to pierce and penetrate through evil. Break the grip of perversion; I speak to the demonic grips of homosexuality and command this book will release captives. I expose truth and release the light of God upon deception. Every demonic agenda and plan I command it to be aborted. I call a technical foul on the enemy for violating and cheating and release the power of God to undue Satan's web. I command the fire of God to burst through darkness and burn every enemy holding my sister and brother in spiritual detention. I command the chains to be broken, the bars to break open, and the captives to be released. I undo wickedness, and I undue and abort demonic agendas. I release the Holy Spirit to draw and summons them to return to their first love. I speak to the sports and entertainment arena, the women in the WNBA who are battling sexual perversion, to be free today. I overthrow demonic stigmas that are linked to women in sports, and declare cleanliness and holiness to permeate the sports and entertainment arena. I prophesy that if you did it for me, You will do it for them. In Jesus' name. Amen.

I pray that my testimony has been a blessing to you. Please share this book with anyone, especially a young person that is struggling or confronted with the issues I address in this book. Remember, "there now no condemnation for those who are in Christ Jesus..." Therefore, it's not about condemnation, but about reconciliation and complete restoration; not by power, nor by might, but by My Spirit saith the Lord. May the grace and peace of our Lord and Savior Jesus Christ, rest, rule and abide in you all.

Though we have come to the end of this book, be encouraged, because joy, hope and a blessed life has just begun!

About the Publisher

Let us bring your story to life! With Life to Legacy, we offer the following publishing services: manuscript development, editing, transcription services, ghostwriting, cover design, copyright services, ISBN assignment, worldwide distribution, and eBook production and distribution.

Throughout the entire production process, you maintain control over your project. We also specialize in family history books, so you can leave a written legacy for your children, grandchildren, and others. You put your story in our hands, and we'll bring it to literary life! We have several publishing packages to meet all your publishing needs.

Call us at: 877-267-7477, or you can also send e-mail to: Life2Legacybooks@att.net. Please visit our Web site:

www.Life2Legacy.com

CPSIA information can be obtained
at www.ICGtesting.com
Printed in the USA
FSOW01n2343221116
27744FS